W9-DDJ-236

Mexican Cookbook

by

Linda Burgett

Creative Ideas Publishing

Second Printing 2004
2,500 Copies

Copyright (2002)
Linda Burgett,
Aztec, New Mexico

Creative Ideas Publishing
PMB 115
2916 N.W. 23rd Street
Bethany, OK 73008-5135
www.busywomanscookbook.com

All Rights Reserved.
No part of this book
may be reproduced in any
form without written
permission from the
publisher, except for brief
passages included
in a review appearing
in a newspaper or
magazine.

ISBN: 1-930170-12-2
Printed in China
Additional copies
may be ordered for
$18.95/each,
plus $3.50 shipping
(tax included).

B & B Books
P.O. Box 1697
Aztec, New Mexico 87410

Order line: 800-673-0768

Cover Design: Laura Gomez
Book Design: Marie Zimmerman

Table of Contents

Special thanks to:

My husband Stan and my son Tyler.
You fill my life with love, joy and laughter.

My mother Sharon McFall and father,
Gene McFall, authors of the best selling
*Busy Women's Cookbook, Cooking With
Will Rogers, Get me out of the Kitchen*, and
Just Around the Curve Cookbook. Their
encouragement and guidance made this
book possible.

My sister and best friend Shelley. Thanks
for always being there.

My brothers Donnie and Scott,
I love you both.

My grandmother and second mom, Marie.

To all my friends and family who shared
their favorite recipes with me.

And most of all to you the reader.
Thanks for bringing me into your kitchen.

Foreword

The blending of cultures over the years has brought many variations to authentic Mexican cooking. Even in Mexico basic recipes vary in the different regions.

Tex-Mex is a term that's used to define the blending of flavors from the southern United States and northern Mexico.

Today Mexican food continues to be changed by a growing number of outside influences. That is what makes Mexican food fun and exciting. There are new dishes and revamps of old dishes constantly being added to menus around the world.

Mexican food is about innovation and experimentation. Do not be afraid to experiment and change Mexican recipes. You may just come up with a new dish.

About the Author

Linda lives in New Mexico with her husband Stan and son Tyler. Her love of different cultures and cuisine makes traveling around the United States and the world as Executive Producer of Passion Play Ministries International a true pleasure. She enjoys entertaining and collecting recipes at the many functions she attends. Her husband's love of spicy Mexican food and her son's desire for mild versions inspired her to write the *Mild to Wild Mexican Cookbook*.

Fire it Up

Appetizers & Dips

Wild Sauce

5 long red or green chile peppers
2 large cloves garlic
1 sprig fresh oregano
1 bay leaf
1 teaspoon salt
1/2 teaspoon cumin seed
2 cups boiling water

Wash and cut slits in chile peppers, do not remove seeds. Peel and slice garlic. In a jar place all ingredients, pouring the boiling water in last. Cover and let stand overnight. Strain out solids; pour Wild Sauce into a glass bottle, chill.

Add to soups and sauces or drizzle over vegetables, chicken or meat.

Makes 2 cups   Extremely Wild & Hot

Every meal in Mexico is served with salsa of some sort.

Kickin' Ketchup

1 cup ketchup
2 tablespoons prepared horseradish
1 tablespoon lemon juice
1/3 cup sweet pickle relish, drained
2 tablespoons finely chopped onion

In a small bowl, combine the ketchup, horseradish, and lemon juice. Add remaining ingredients, mix well. Chill for at least 1 hour.

Makes 1 1/2 cups   Wild & Hot

Hot Flashes Salsa

1 (14¹/₂ ounce) can tomato wedges
1 onion, finely diced
1 (4 ounce) can chopped Jalapeno peppers
1 tablespoon finely cut fresh cilantro

In a medium bowl pour tomatoes and crush until small pieces remain. Add remaining ingredients and mix. Chill for 1 hour.

Makes 2¹/₂ cups   Wild & Hot

Mild Version: Use mild chile peppers and decrease the amount to 2 ounces.

Sassy Salsa

6 tomatoes, chopped
6 Jalapeno peppers, seeded and chopped
3 green onions, chopped with the tops
1 diced red onion
1 (8 ounce) can tomato sauce
1 (4 ounce) can diced hot green chiles
2 tablespoons vinegar
¹/₂ teaspoon salt
1 tablespoon minced cilantro
¹/₂ teaspoon oregano
¹/₂ teaspoon chili powder
¹/₄ teaspoon cumin powder
¹/₄ teaspoon garlic powder

In a medium bowl, combine all ingredients. Chill at least three hours.

Makes 6 cups   Wild & Hot

Mild Version: Reduce the Jalapeno peppers to one.

In a recent survey, salsa was voted number one condiment.

Mediterranean Salsa

6 cloves garlic, minced
1/4 cup chopped fine onion
3 tablespoons olive oil
4 tomatoes, seeded and chopped
24 green olives, chopped fine
2 long green chiles, seeded and chopped
1 1/2 tablespoons red wine vinegar
2 teaspoons Cayenne pepper
1/2 teaspoon salt
1/2 teaspoon ground cumin

In a large saucepan, sauté garlic and onion in olive oil over medium high heat until golden brown. Add remaining ingredients. Bring to a boil. Reduce heat and simmer 5 minutes. Chill 2 hours before serving.

Make 3 cups   Medium

What is hot? Each person is different. What is mild to one will taste hot to another.

Rojo Salsa

1 (8 ounce) can tomato sauce
1 (14 1/2 ounce) can diced tomatoes
1/2 green pepper, chopped
2 bunches green onion, chopped
1 (14 1/2 ounce) can diced green chiles
1 teaspoon garlic powder
2 teaspoons sugar
2 tablespoons minced cilantro
1 1/2 teaspoons cumin
1/2 teaspoon crushed red pepper
Salt to taste

In a large bowl, combine all ingredients together and chill.

Makes 6 cups   Medium

Mild Version: Do not add red pepper and add only 1/2 teaspoon cumin.

11

Green With Envy Salsa

1 cup chopped onions
1/4 cup vegetable oil
1 1/2 cups of whole canned green tomatillos,
  with liquid
1 1/2 cups chopped spinach
1 (4 ounce) can green chiles, drained
2 cloves garlic, minced
1 tablespoon oregano
1 cup chicken broth

In a large saucepan, brown onions in oil.
Add tomatillos, spinach, garlic, and oregano.
Cover and cook over medium heat for five
minutes. Cool slightly. Pour mixture into a
blender. Add green chiles. Blend on low speed
until smooth. Return to sauce pan and stir in
chicken broth. Heat to boiling then reduce and
simmer uncovered 15 minutes. Cool and chill.

Makes 5 1/2 cups   Mild

Removing the seeds in a pepper is an easy way to control the heat of the recipe.

Double Trouble Salsa

1 (10 ounce) can chopped tomatoes
  and green chiles
4 green onions, chopped, including tops
2 Jalapeno peppers, chopped
1 Cayenne pepper, chopped
1 teaspoon chopped cilantro
1 teaspoon chopped fine garlic
  salt to taste

Combine all ingredients in a blender. Cover,
blend until smooth. Chill and serve.

Makes 4 cups   Wild & Hot

*Mild Version: Replace Jalapeno peppers with 1
(4 ounce) can chopped green chiles. Eliminate
Cayenne pepper.*

Salsa with A Bite

1 large onion, chopped
4 Jalapeno peppers, chopped
1 large green pepper, chopped
1 teaspoon vegetable oil
1 (28 ounce) can tomatoes, chopped
$1/2$ cup tomato sauce
1 teaspoon cumin
1 teaspoon oregano
1 teaspoon sugar
$1/2$ teaspoon garlic powder
$1/2$ teaspoon salt

In a large saucepan over medium heat, brown onion and peppers in oil. Add remaining ingredients. Reduce heat, cover and simmer for 10 minutes. Chill before serving.

Makes 6 cups   Wild & Hot

Mild Version: Replace Jalapeno peppers with mild green chiles. Reduce cumin to $1/4$ teaspoon.

 Wear plastic gloves while handling and preparing Jalapeno peppers.

Black Bean Salsa

5 Jalapeno peppers, pealed, seeded,
    and chopped
2 (15 ounce) cans black beans, rinsed
    and drained
2 cups corn
1 cup seeded and chopped tomato
1 red pepper, seeded and chopped
1 red onion, chopped
1 clove garlic, minced
1/3 cup lime juice
2 tablespoons cilantro, minced

In a medium bowl, combine all ingredients.
Cover and chill for at least 2 hours.

Makes 12 servings   Wild & Hot

*Mild Version: Reduce Jalapeno peppers to
1/2 of one Jalapeno pepper.*

Peppers picked in the hottest summer month will be hotter then the ones you pick in the early summer or fall.

Bites Back Salsa

4 tomatoes, chopped
2 (4 ounce) cans hot green chiles, chopped
2 (4 ounce) cans chopped black olives,
    drained
5 green onions, chopped with tops
1 tablespoon white vinegar
1/4 teaspoon salt

In a medium bowl, combine all ingredients
together. Chill for at least two hours before
serving.

Makes 4 cups   Wild & Hot

*Mild Version: Use only one can of mild
green chiles.*

Macho Mango Salsa

1 large mango, peeled and cut into
  1/4 inch cubes
1 Jalapeno pepper, seeded and diced
1/4 cup red bell pepper, diced
2 teaspoons lime juice
1 1/2 teaspoons red wine vinegar
1/2 teaspoons sugar

In a medium bowl, combine all ingredients.
Mix well. Refrigerate 1 hour before serving.

Makes 4 servings   Medium

Aloha Salsa

2 tomatoes, chopped
2 green onions with tops, chopped
1 cucumber, seeded and diced
1 New Mexican chile, chopped
1/2 cup pineapple tidbits
1/4 cup chopped cilantro
2 tablespoons lime juice
1 tablespoon white wine vinegar
1 tablespoon oil
1/2 teaspoon salt

In a medium bowl, combine all ingredients
until well blended. Cover and chill at least
one hour.

Makes 4 cups   Medium

How to Pick a Pepper: Peppers that are red are hotter than green or yellow peppers. The hottest peppers have pointed tips and narrow tops. Round ends indicate mildness. Of course to every rule there is an exception. The fiery Habanero pepper is rounded and often green or yellow in color.

Pico de Gallo Salsa

1 cup finely chopped tomatoes
1/3 cup finely chopped onion
2 Jalapeno peppers, chopped
1 Serrano pepper, chopped
2 cloves garlic, minced
2 tablespoons lime juice
1 tablespoon chopped cilantro
1/4 teaspoon salt

In medium bowl, combine all ingredients. Chill for at least 30 minutes before serving.

Makes 2 cups   Wild & Hot

Mild Version: Eliminate the Jalapeno peppers. Reduce garlic to 1 clove.

Restaurant Style Salsa

1 cup finely chopped fresh tomatoes
1 (4 ounce) can chopped green chiles
3 tablespoons finely chopped green onion
1 tablespoon finely chopped cilantro
1 1/2 teaspoons lemon juice
2 teaspoons hot pepper sauce
1 teaspoon finely chopped garlic
1/4 teaspoon ground cumin
1/4 teaspoon salt

Combine all ingredients in blender. Cover, blend until it reaches the consistency you desire. Chill at least 1 hour.

Makes 1 1/4 cups   Medium

Garlic cloves will never dry out if you store them in a bottle of cooking oil. After the garlic is used up, you can use the garlic flavored oil as salad dressing.

Fire Engine Salsa

2 cups finely chopped plum tomatoes
1/2 cup chicken broth
1/2 cup finely chopped white onions
5 Ancho chiles, chopped
2 tablespoons finely chopped cilantro
1 tablespoon lime juice
1 tablespoon olive oil
1 clove garlic, minced
1/4 teaspoon salt

In a large saucepan, combine all ingredients. Bring to a boil, reduce heat and simmer for 10 minutes. Stir frequently. Serve warm or cold.

Makes 4 cups   Wild & Hot

Mild Version: Reduce Ancho peppers to 1 pepper.

The longer garlic cooks, the milder the flavor.

Habanero Salsa

1 (20 ounce) can chopped tomatoes
4 green onions, chopped with the tops
3 cloves garlic, minced
1 tablespoon chopped cilantro
1 tablespoon lime juice
1 teaspoon vinegar
2 Habanero peppers, pureed
1/4 teaspoon salt

In a medium bowl, combine all ingredients. Cover and chill over night.

Makes 3 cups   Wild & Hot

Some Like it Hot Salsa

2 large tomatoes, diced
3 Jalapeno peppers, finely chopped
1/2 cup chopped onion
2 tablespoons chopped cilantro
2 tablespoons lime juice
1 clove garlic, minced
1 teaspoon olive oil
3/4 teaspoon salt
1/2 teaspoon cumin
1/4 teaspoon black pepper

In a medium bowl, combine all ingredients. Chill for 2 hours. Serve with tortilla chips.

Makes 1 1/2 cups   Wild & Hot

Hot peppers are believed to have healing power.

More Bark Than Bite Salsa

1 (28 ounce) can diced tomatoes
1 (8 ounce) can tomato sauce
1 (4 ounce) can diced hot green chiles
1 bunch green onions with tops, chopped
1/2 green pepper, chopped
1 tablespoon minced cilantro
2 teaspoons crushed red pepper
2 teaspoons sugar
1 teaspoon garlic powder
1 teaspoon cumin
1 teaspoon salt

In a large bowl, combine all ingredients, mix well. Chill at least 4 hours.

Makes 6 cups   Medium

Mild Version: Use a can of mild chiles instead of the hot chiles. Reduce red pepper to 1/2 teaspoon.

White Hot Salsa

1 cup Ranch salad dressing
1/2 cup milk
2 tablespoons sour cream
1/2 tablespoon minced garlic
1 1/2 teaspoons ground red pepper flakes
1 1/2 teaspoons cumin
1 1/2 teaspoons oregano

In a small bowl, combine all ingredients, mix well. Cover and chill for at least 3 hours.

Makes 4 servings   Medium

Mild Version: Reduce cumin and red pepper flakes to 1/2 teaspoon.

Green peppers are a source of vitamin C, red peppers are a source of vitamin A.

Guacamole

3 ripe avocados, peeled and diced
1 tomato, diced
1/2 onion, diced
1 1/2 tablespoons lemon juice
2 Jalapeno peppers, seeded and minced
1 clove garlic, minced
1/4 teaspoon salt

In a large bowl mash avocados. Add remaining ingredients, mix well. Chill 1 hour. Serve with tortilla chips.

Makes 2 cups   Wild & Hot

Mild Version: Eliminate Jalapeno peppers. Add 1 tablespoon diced mild green chile.

Spicy Guacamole

1/4 cup chopped onion
1 clove garlic, minced
2 teaspoons cumin
2 teaspoons chili powder
2 cups frozen peas
1/3 cup water
1/4 cup chopped avocado
1/4 cup diced tomato
1/2 teaspoon salt
1/2 teaspoon black pepper

In a large non-stick skillet over medium heat, cook onion, garlic, cumin, and chili powder until onion is tender. Add peas and water; cook an additional 3 minutes. Pour cooked mixture into blender, puree until smooth. Let cool and add remaining ingredients, mix well. Serve with tortilla chips.

Makes 5 servings   Medium

Peppers contain more vitamin A and C than orange juice.

Pronto Guacamole

2 large ripe avocados, peeled and seeded
1/2 cup Picante Sauce
2 teaspoons lemon juice
1/2 teaspoon salt

In a small bowl, mash avocados. Add Picante Sauce, lemon juice, and salt, mix well.

Makes 2 cups   Mild

Chile con Queso Dip

2 tablespoons butter
2 green peppers, seeded and chopped
1 red pepper, seeded and chopped
1 small onion, chopped
2 (8 ounce) packages of cream cheese,
    softened
1/2 teaspoon pepper sauce
1/4 teaspoon salt

In a large saucepan, melt butter over medium heat. Add peppers and onion; sauté until onion is transparent. Mix in cream cheese, pepper sauce, and salt. Reduce heat to low and simmer for 15 minutes. Serve warm.

Makes 8 servings   Medium

Senorita's Chile con Queso

1 tablespoon vegetable oil
1/2 cup diced onion
1 (15 ounce) can tomatoes and chile
2 tablespoons milk
2 pound block of processed cheese,
    cut into small squares

In a large skillet on high heat, add oil and onions, sauté until onions are transparent. Add tomatoes and chile to mixture; add milk. Heat to a boil, reduce heat to low, add cheese, stirring constantly. Serve warm with tortilla chips or fresh vegetables.

Makes 7 cups   Medium

Cut and pit an avocado with the skin on. Then use a spoon to scoop the avocado out of the skin

Chile con Queso with Mayo

2 tablespoons mayonnaise
1 onion, finely diced
2 pound block of processed cheese, cubed
1 (8 ounce) can evaporated milk
1 (8 ounce) can diced green chiles

In a large skillet over medium high heat, sauté mayonnaise and onions. Add cheese slowly, stirring constantly. After the cheese has melted, add milk and chiles. Serve warm with tortilla chips.

Makes 7 cups   Medium

The Red Savina Habanero pepper is the hottest pepper known.

Quick Queso

2 pound block of Velveeta® cheese
2 cups thick and chunky salsa

In a 2 quart microwavable bowl, cut up Velveeta® cheese into small pieces. Microwave on high for 5 minutes or until cheese has melted. Blend salsa into cheese, microwave an additional minute. Serve warm with tortilla chips or fresh vegetables.

Makes 6 cups   Mild

Fired Up Cheese Dip

1 pound Mexican Velveeta® cheese, cubed
1 (15 ounce) can chili without beans
1/4 cup hot salsa
Dash of hot pepper sauce

In a medium saucepan over medium low heat, melt cheese. Add remaining ingredients, mix well. Serve warm with your favorite corn chips.

Makes 3 cups   Wild & Hot

Mild Version: Use regular Velveeta® cheese, mild salsa and eliminate the hot pepper sauce.

Dos Cheese Dip

1/2 cup chopped onions
1 (4 ounce) can green chiles, chopped
2 tablespoons butter or margarine
2 tablespoons flour
1/2 cup milk
1 1/2 cups Velveeta® cheese, cubed
1 cup Monterey Jack cheese
1/2 cup chopped tomato

In a 2 quart saucepan over medium heat, add onions, green chiles, and butter. When butter is melted, stir in flour until smooth. Gradually stir in milk, blend well, cook until thickened. Add cheeses and tomato; cook until cheese is melted. Serve warm with tortilla chips.

Makes 4 1/2 cups   Medium

 One way to keep from getting bored when on a diet, is to spice your food well. Stock up on Mexican spices and salsa.

Gringo Cheese Dip

2 tablespoons butter
2 tablespoons flour
1 cup milk
7 processed American Cheese slices
$1/2$ teaspoon salt

In a medium saucepan, melt butter over medium heat. Stir in flour. Pour in milk, stir until thickens. Add cheese and salt; stir constantly until cheese has melted completely.

Makes $1^1/2$ cups   Mild

Azul Cheese Dip

$1^1/2$ cups sour cream
$1/2$ cup crumbled blue cheese
2 tablespoons green onions,
   chopped without the tops
1 garlic clove, minced
$1/4$ teaspoon hot pepper sauce

In a small bowl, combine sour cream and blue cheese. Add remaining ingredients, mix well. Refrigerate for at least 2 hours.

Makes 2 cups   Medium

As tomato paste cooks, the natural sugars caramelize, creating a deep rich flavor.

Frijol Dip

1 (16 ounce) can refried beans

1/2 teaspoon chili powder

2 avocados, peeled and mashed

1/2 cup mayonnaise

6 strips of bacon, crisp and crumbled

1/2 cup chopped onion

1/2 teaspoon salt

1 (14 ounce) can chopped green chiles,
   drained

2 cups shredded Monterey Jack cheese

1 cup chopped black olives

1 cup chopped tomato

In a small bowl, blend refried beans and chili powder. Spread in 9 x 13 inch pan. In a small bowl, combine avocado, mayonnaise, bacon, onion, and salt. Layer on top of bean mixture. Top with green chiles, cheese, olives, and tomato in layers. Serve with tortilla chips or crackers.

Makes 24 servings   Mild

Peppers
were first
grown
by the Aztecs.

Explosive Two Bean Dip

1 (16 ounce) can Great Northern beans, drained
3 tablespoons grated Parmesan cheese
1/2 cup chopped onion, divided
1/2 teaspoon salt, divided
1/2 teaspoon black pepper, divided
2 cloves garlic, minced and divided
1 (15 ounce) can black beans, drained
1 (4 ounce) can chopped green chiles, drained
1/4 teaspoon cumin
1 cup shredded cheddar cheese

In a large bowl, combine Great Northern beans, Parmesan cheese, 1/4 cup onion, 1/4 teaspoon of salt and pepper, 1 clove of garlic. Mix with an electric mixer until smooth. Spoon into an 8 x 8 baking dish. In a large bowl, combine black beans, 1/4 cup onion, 1/4 teaspoon of salt and pepper, 1 clove of garlic, chiles, cumin. Mix with an electric mixer until smooth. Spoon over top of Great Northern bean mixture. Sprinkle with cheese. Serve with tortilla chips.

Makes 12 servings   Medium

Mild Version: Eliminate green chiles.

A crock pot makes an ideal serving container for hot punch or hot dip.

Double Cheese Bean Dip

Preheat Oven to 350 degrees

1 (8 ounce) package cream cheese, softened
1 cup sour cream
1/2 (1 ounce) package taco seasoning mix
2 tablespoons dried parsley
1/2 cup chopped green onions
10 drops hot pepper sauce
2 (16 ounce) cans refried beans
1 (8 ounce) package shredded cheddar cheese
1 (8 ounce) package shredded Monterey Jack cheese

In a medium bowl, combine cream cheese and sour cream. Mix in taco seasoning, parsley, green onions, and hot pepper sauce. Blend refried beans into cream cheese mixture, mix well. Add half of the cheddar and half of the Monterey cheeses to the refried beans and cream cheese mixture, mix well. Spread mixture into an 8 x 12 inch lightly greased baking dish. Top with remaining cheese. Bake for 20 minutes or until the cheese is melted.

Makes 12 cups   Medium

Spanish priests believed chiles were an aphrodisiac. They warned against consumption, which probably added to their popularity.

Spicy Spinach Dip

Preheat Oven to 400 degrees

1 (10 ounce) package frozen chopped
  spinach, thawed and drained
1 (16 ounce) jar salsa
2 cups shredded Monterey Jack cheese
1 (8 ounce) package cream cheese,
  room temperature
1 cup evaporated milk
1 ($2^1/4$ ounce) can chopped black olives,
  drained
1 tablespoon red wine vinegar
$1/4$ teaspoon salt
$1/4$ teaspoon black pepper

In a large bowl, combine all ingredients.
Pour into an 8 x 8 inch baking dish. Bake
for 15 minutes.

Makes 12 servings   Mild

Indian
tribes
strung
chiles together
and hung
them from their
canoes to
ward off evils
in the water.

Caliente Spinach Dip

2 pounds pepper jack cheese, cubed
2 cups half and half cream
3 cups chopped spinach, rinsed
1 tomato, chopped
1 onion, diced
$1/2$ cup diced red pepper

In a double broiler, slowly melt pepper jack
cheese. When cheese is almost completely
melted add half and half, whisk until cheese is
completely melted. Stir in spinach, tomato,
onion, and red pepper, cook 1 minute. Serve
warm with tortilla chips.

Makes 12 servings   Mild

Jalapeno Dip

5 Jalapeno peppers, seeded and
  chopped
1 onion, chopped
16 ounces Velveeta® cheese, diced
2 cups mayonnaise

In a blender, puree Jalapeno peppers. Add onion and cheese, blend until smooth. Add mayonnaise, blend completely. Serve with tortilla chips.

Makes 24 servings   Wild & Hot

Mild Version: Use 1 Jalapeno pepper and one green pepper seeded and chopped.

Baked Jalapeno Dip

Preheat Oven to 350 degrees

8 ounces cheddar cheese, shredded
1 cup mayonnaise
1 (4 ounce) can diced Jalapeno peppers
1 (2 ounce) can diced black olives
1/2 teaspoon garlic salt
2 drops hot pepper sauce
1 tomato, chopped
1/2 cup chopped green onions, with tops

In a medium size bowl, combine cheddar cheese, mayonnaise, half each of Jalapeno peppers, black olives, garlic salt, hot pepper sauce. Spread mixture into a lightly greased 8 x 8 inch baking dish. Bake for 20 to 25 minutes. Before serving top with remaining Jalapeno peppers, black olives, tomato, and green onions.

Makes 10 servings   Medium

Guam is the world's largest consumer of Tabasco sauce.

Chicken Enchilada Dip

Preheat Oven to 350 degrees

1 pound chicken breast meat,
  cooked and shredded
1 (8 ounce) jar mayonnaise
1 (8 ounce) package cream cheese, softened
1 (4 ounce) can diced green chiles
1 Jalapeno pepper, chopped finely
1 (16 ounce) package cheddar cheese,
  shredded

In a medium bowl, combine chicken, mayonnaise, cream cheese, green chiles, and Jalapeno pepper. Spread in a 9 x 13 inch baking dish. Top with cheddar cheese. Bake for 30 minutes or until cheese is melted. Serve with crackers or tortilla chips.

Makes 30 servings   Mild

George Washington and Thomas Jefferson, are both known to have grown chiles.

Chi Chi Dip

2 chicken breasts, cooked and shredded
2 (8 ounce) packages cream cheese, softened
1 1/2 cups shredded Monterey Jack cheese
3 Jalapeno peppers, seeded, chopped finely
3 tablespoons onion, minced finely
2 cloves garlic, minced
1 teaspoon chili powder
1 teaspoon ground cumin
1/4 teaspoon pepper
1/4 teaspoon salt

In a medium bowl, combine all ingredients, mix well. Spread in an 8 x 8 inch dish. Serve with crackers or tortilla chips.

Makes 3 cups   Wild & Hot

Mild Version: Eliminate Jalapeno peppers, add 1 (4 ounce) can green chiles.

Sombrero Dip

1 pound bacon, cooked and crumbled
1 (8 ounce) package cream cheese,
  softened
1 cup sour cream
4 tomatoes, chopped
4 green onions with tops, chopped
1 green pepper, chopped
1 (16 ounce) jar salsa
2 cups shredded cheddar cheese

In a large frying pan, cook bacon until crisp.
Drain on paper towel, set aside. In a medium
bowl, mix cream cheese and sour cream with
a hand mixer. Spread cream cheese mixture
into a 9 X 13 inch pan. In a medium bowl,
mix tomatoes, green onions, and green
pepper. Layer onto the cream cheese mixture.
Pour salsa over the vegetables, coating
evenly. Sprinkle cheddar cheese over top
of salsa. Crumble the bacon over cheddar
cheese. Chill at least 1 hour.

Makes 12 servings   Mild

The best relief for a burning mouth is sour cream or yogurt.

Taco Salad Dip

1¹/2 pounds ground beef
1 (1 ounce) package taco seasoning
¹/2 cup water
2 (8 ounce) packages cream cheese, softened
¹/4 cup milk
1¹/2 cups chopped lettuce
1 cup chopped onions
2 tomatoes, chopped
1 (4 ounce) diced green chiles, drained
¹/2 cup honey barbecue sauce
1¹/2 cups shredded cheddar cheese

In a large skillet over medium high heat, brown ground beef, drain off grease. Add taco seasoning and water, reduce heat and simmer for 5 minutes. In a small bowl blend cream cheese and milk until well mixed. Spread mixture evenly on a serving platter or large plate. Layer beef, lettuce, onions, tomatoes, green chiles, over cream cheese mixture. Drizzle the barbecue sauce over layers. Top with cheddar cheese. Serve with corn chips.

Makes 10 servings   Mild

Use a green bell pepper (cut off top and remove seeds) as a dish to hold salsa or other dips.

Green Chile Dip

2 cups sour cream
1 (4 ounce) can hot diced green chiles
¹/2 cup chopped tomato

In a medium bowl, combine all ingredients, mix well. Chill at least 2 hours.

Makes 2³/4 cups   Medium

Mild Version: Use mild green chile. For a very mild taste use only 2 ounces of green chiles, increase the amount of tomato by 3 tablespoons.

El Pan Dip

Preheat oven to 350 degrees

1¹/2 cups shredded cheddar cheese
1 (8 ounce) package cream cheese
1 cup sour cream
1 cup salsa
1 (1 pound) round loaf Italian bread

In a medium bowl, combine cheddar cheese, cream cheese, sour cream, and salsa. Cut the top of the bread off of loaf. Scoop out the inside and tear into bite size pieces, set aside. Spoon the cheese mixture into bread bowl; place top back on the loaf. Wrap in aluminum foil. Bake for 1¹/2 hours. Serve warm with the bread pieces.

Makes 8 servings   Mild

Salsa is the Spanish word for sauce.

Layered Dip

2 (8 ounce) packages of cream cheese, room temperature
2 (16 ounce) jars salsa
2 tomatoes, chopped
2 green peppers, chopped
1 cup chopped Jalapeno peppers
1 (4 ounce) can chopped black olives, drained
16 ounces shredded cheddar cheese

In a medium bowl, mix until smooth, cream cheese and 1 jar of salsa. Spread evenly in an 8 x 8 inch baking dish. Top with remaining salsa. Sprinkle tomato, green pepper, Jalapeno peppers, and black olives, over salsa. Top with cheese. Serve with tortilla chips

Makes 6 cups   Wild & Hot

Mild Version: *Eliminate Jalapeno peppers. Replace salsa with an equal amount of chopped tomato.*

Avocado Layered Dip

1 cup sour cream
1/2 cup mayonnaise
1 (1.5 ounce) package taco seasoning
3 avocados
2 teaspoons lemon juice
1/2 teaspoon salt
1/4 teaspoon pepper
1 (10 ounce) can refried beans
1 (4 ounce) can hot diced green chiles
1/2 cup chopped green onions, with tops
2 tomatoes, chopped
8 ounces cheddar cheese, shredded

In a small bowl, combine the sour cream, mayonnaise, and taco seasoning. Spread mixture into an 8 X 8 inch pan. In a separate small bowl, mash avocados with the lemon juice, salt, and pepper. Spread over sour cream mixture. In a small bowl, mash the refried beans. You may need to add a small amount of water to the beans in order to make it easy to spread. Spread beans on top of avocado mixture. Sprinkle the green chiles, onions, and tomatoes over beans. Top with shredded cheese.

Makes 12 servings   Medium

Mild Version: *Eliminate the green chiles. Use 1 green pepper, seeded and chopped.*

More than 140 varieties of chiles are grown in Mexico.

Layered Pumpkin Dip

1 (15 ounce) can pumpkin
1 (8 ounce) package cream cheese,
   softened
1 (8 ounce) container sour cream
2 tablespoons finely chopped Jalapeno
   peppers,
1 (4 ounce) can diced green chiles
1/2 teaspoon garlic salt
1 tomato, chopped
3 green onions, chopped with tops
1 (2.25 ounce) can sliced black olives

In a medium bowl, combine pumpkin and
cream cheese. Spread mixture into an 8 x 8
inch pan. In a small bowl, combine sour
cream, jalapenoes, chiles, and garlic salt.
Spread over pumpkin mixture. Top with
tomato, onions, and black olives. Cover and
chill for 2 hours. Serve with tortilla chips.

Makes 12 servings   Mild

 Jalapeno peppers are the most widely used pepper in the United States. The Serrano pepper is in second place.

Scoop Dip

2 (8 ounce) packages cream cheese,
   softened
1 (16 ounce) container sour cream
1 (16 ounce) jar thick and chunky salsa
10 ounces shredded cheddar cheese
1 (5.75 ounce) can black olives, chopped

In a medium bowl using a mixer, combine
cream cheese and sour cream until smooth.
Spread cream cheese mixture into a 9 X 13
inch pan, coating the pan evenly. Sprinkle
shredded cheese over top of cream cheese
mixture, followed by the black olives.

Makes 9 servings   Mild

Eat the Dish Dip

Preheat oven to 350 degrees

1 (1 pound) loaf round bread
1 (8 ounce) cream cheese, room temperature
1 (8 ounce) package shredded cheddar cheese
1½ cups sour cream
½ cup chopped green onions
⅓ cup chopped green chiles
1 (4 ounce) jar dried beef, chopped
½ teaspoon Worcestershire sauce

Cut off the top of the loaf. Scoop out bread, leaving a hollow shell. Set aside top of bread and removed pieces. In a medium bowl, mix the remaining ingredients. Spoon mixture into the loaf. Replace top of bread. Wrap in foil and bake for 90 minutes. Serve with scooped out bread and crackers.

Makes 12 servings   Medium

Mild Version: *Eliminate green chiles, replace with ¼ cup mild salsa.*

When a Jalapeno pepper is smoked it becomes a Chipotle chile.

Bell Pepper Dip

4 green onions with tops, chopped
2 green bell peppers, chopped
1 red bell pepper, chopped
2 tablespoons butter
2 (8 ounce) package cream cheese, softened
½ teaspoon chile sauce

In a large saucepan over medium to high heat, sauté onions and peppers in butter. Cook until onions are transparent. Add cream cheese and chile sauce. Reduce heat, simmer 15 minutes. Serve warm.

Makes 6 servings   Mild

Baked Crab Dip

Preheat oven to 350 degrees

1 (8 ounce) package cream cheese, room temperature
1 cup salsa
1 teaspoon chili powder
8 ounces imitation crab meat
1 cup shredded cheddar cheese
1/4 cup sliced black olives

Spread cream cheese in a 9 inch pie pan. In a small bowl, mix salsa and chili powder, spoon over cream cheese. Layer crabmeat, cheese, and black olives. Bake for 15 minutes. Serve with tortilla chips or crackers.

Makes 8 servings   Medium

Mild Version: Reduce chili powder to 1/4 teaspoon and use mild salsa.

Cheesy Crab Dip

1 (8 ounce) package cream cheese, softened
1 cup salsa
8 ounces imitation crabmeat, softened
1 cup shredded cheddar cheese
1/3 cup chopped green onions
2 tablespoons diced tomato
2 tablespoons sliced black olives

In a medium bowl, combine cream cheese and salsa. Add crabmeat, cheese, and onions, mix well. Place in a serving bowl and top with tomatoes and black olives. Serve with crackers or chips.

Makes 3 cups   Mild

The Ancho is a dried Pablano pepper. It is the most popular dried pepper in the US and Mexico. With its slightly fruity flavor, the Ancho is the sweetest dried pepper.

Clam With a Kick Dip

1 (8 ounce) package cream cheese
1/4 cup sour cream
1 tablespoon chile sauce
1 teaspoon lemon juice
1 teaspoon hot pepper sauce
1/4 teaspoon Worcestershire sauce
1/2 cup canned clams, drained
1 tablespoon finely chopped onion

In a medium bowl, using a mixer, combine cream cheese and sour cream. Add chile sauce, lemon juice, hot pepper sauce, and Worcestershire sauce, mix well. Add clams and onions, mix well. Chill at least 1 hour before serving.

Makes 12 servings   Wild & Hot

Mild Version: Reduce chile sauce to 1/2 teaspoon and hot pepper sauce to 1/4 teaspoon.

Rapido Salsa Dip

2 cups sour cream
1 cup salsa
tortilla chips

In a small bowl, combine sour cream and salsa. Cover and chill for 2 hours. Serve with tortilla chips.

Makes 3 cups   Mild

Chipotle pepper is a ripened and smoked Jalapeno pepper. Its smoky flavor is fiery hot.

Hot Tamale Dip

Preheat oven to 350 degrees

2 (14$^{1}/_{2}$ ounce) cans tamales
1 (15 ounce) can chile con carne
$^{1}/_{2}$ cup onion, chopped finely
1 pound cheddar cheese, shredded
$^{1}/_{2}$ cup salsa

Remove wrappers from tamales and cut into medium size pieces, place in a 2 quart baking dish. Spread chile con carne over tamales. Sprinkle onions over chile con carne. Cover with cheddar cheese. Bake for 30 minutes or until cheese is lightly browned. Top with salsa.

Makes 15 servings   Medium

Cilantro Dip

1 (8 ounce) package of cream cheese, softened
1 (7 ounce) can tomatillo salsa
1 tablespoon sour cream
1 tablespoon lime juice
1 bunch cilantro, chopped
2 teaspoons garlic powder
1 teaspoon black pepper
1 teaspoon celery salt
$^{1}/_{2}$ teaspoon ground cumin

In a blender, puree cream cheese, salsa, sour cream, and lime juice. Add cilantro, garlic powder, pepper, celery salt, and cumin, blend until smooth and creamy. Serve with tortilla chips.

Makes 12 servings   Mild

 Commercial chili powder is made from ground red chile and a variety of other spices

Fiesta Fruit Dip

1 (8 ounce) package cream cheese
2 1/2 tablespoons vanilla yogurt
1/4 cup brown sugar, lightly packed
1 1/2 teaspoons vanilla extract

In a medium bowl combine all ingredients, mix well. Serve with Cinnamon Crisps or apple slices.

Makes 4 servings   Mild

Cinnamon Crisps

Preheat oven to 350 degrees

1 tablespoon sugar
1/4 teaspoon cinnamon
2 (8 inch) flour tortillas
1 tablespoon water

In a small bowl, combine sugar and cinnamon. Brush both sides of tortillas with water; sprinkle each side with sugar mixture. Cut tortilla into 12 wedges. Place on a cookie sheet in a single layer. Bake for 15 minutes.

Makes 6 servings   Mild

Chili Chips

6 (8 inch) flour tortillas
2 teaspoons vegetable oil
2 teaspoons chili powder
2 teaspoons cumin

Cut each tortilla into 8 wedges. In a small bowl combine oil, chili powder, and cumin. Brush oil mixture on both sides of tortillas; place on a cookie sheet in one layer. Broil for 6 minutes, turn half way through.

Makes 6 servings   Medium

Some research suggests that eating chile peppers may help keep your metabolism healthfully high.

Chili Popcorn

3 quarts popped popcorn
2 tablespoons butter or margarine,
  melted
1 tablespoon Dijon mustard
2 teaspoons chili powder
$1/4$ teaspoon ground cumin
$1/4$ teaspoon salt

In a large bowl, place popcorn. In a small
bowl combine all remaining ingredients.
Pour butter mixture over popcorn and
toss until coated.

Makes 3 quarts   Medium

Peppy Pretzels

Preheat oven to 200 degrees

1 (20 ounce) bag mini pretzels
1 (1.6 ounces) package dry ranch
  dressing
1 teaspoon Cayenne pepper
1 teaspoon garlic salt
1 cup vegetable oil

In a small bowl, combine all ingredients
except pretzels. Place pretzels in a large
roasting pan. Pour mixed ingredients over
pretzels stirring to coat completely. Bake
uncovered for 1 hour, stirring every
20 minutes.

Makes 10 servings   Medium

 Salsas
are low in
  calories,
cholesterol,
and fat. They
add extra
flavor to
almost any
dish.

Taco Crunch

Preheat oven to 350 degrees

1/2 cup butter or margarine
1 (1.25 ounce) package taco seasoning
8 cups square shaped corn cereal

Melt butter in a 9 x 13 inch baking pan by putting it in the oven for 3 minutes. Remove and stir in taco seasoning, mix well. Add cereal; coat evenly with butter mixture. Bake for 10 minutes or until cereal is crispy.

Makes 8 cups   Mild

Jalapeno Poppers

1 (3.5 ounce) can Jalapeno peppers, drained
1 cup shredded cheddar cheese
1/4 cup cilantro, chopped
3 ounces cream cheese, softened
1/2 cup flour
2 eggs, beaten
2 cups crushed corn flakes cereal

Cut a slit lengthwise in each Jalapeno pepper, remove seeds. In a small bowl, combine cheddar cheese, cilantro, and cream cheese. Stuff each pepper with 1 to 1 1/2 teaspoon cheese mixture, chill for 20 minutes. Dip each pepper in flour, shake off excess. Dip in egg next then roll in corn flakes. In a medium size skillet heat 1 inch of vegetable oil over high heat. Fry Jalapeno pepper, turning to brown each side. Fry until golden brown. Drain on paper towel. Serve while still warm.

Makes 8 servings   Wild & Hot

To check if your chile powder is still fresh, pinch a small amount between your fingers. If it sticks together, there is still oil in the powder and it is ready to be used. If it does not stick together, it will no longer have the desired taste.

Mex Mix

Preheat oven to 350 degrees

1/2 cup butter or margarine
1 (1.25) package taco seasoning
3 cups square rice cereal
3 cups corn chips
3 cups lightly salted peanuts
2 cups lightly salted pretzels

In a 9 x 13 inch baking pan, melt butter in oven for 3 minutes. Add taco seasoning, mix well. Combine rice cereal, corn chips, peanuts, and pretzels, toss to coat. Bake for 20 minutes or until crispy.

Makes 20 servings   Mild

Peppers are a fruit, not a vegetable.

Jalapeno Slices

1 cup flour
1 teaspoon chili powder
1 teaspoon garlic powder
1 teaspoon salt
1 teaspoon black pepper
2 eggs
1 cup water
2 cups sliced Jalapeno peppers
1/2 quart vegetable oil

In a medium bowl combine flour, chili powder, garlic powder, salt, and black pepper. Add eggs and water, mix well. Heat oil in a large sauce pan or deep fryer to 365 degrees. Dip Jalapeno slices into batter, place in hot oil. Cook until golden brown. Serve warm.

Makes 4 servings   Wild & Hot

Fiery Fried Jalapenos

1 cup flour
2 teaspoons garlic salt
1 teaspoon Tabasco® sauce
1 cup water
2 eggs
2 cups sliced Jalapeno peppers

Mix flour, garlic salt, Tabasco, water, and eggs in a medium size bowl. Heat the oil to 365 degrees in a deep fryer or a large saucepan. Dip sliced Jalapenos in the batter and place in the oil. Jalapenos are fully cooked when they float to the surface of the oil and are golden brown and crispy.

Makes 6 servings   Wild & Hot

Taco Cups

Preheat oven to 400 degrees

1 pound ground beef
1 (1.25 ounce) package taco seasoning
1 (10 ounce) can refrigerator buttermilk
   biscuits
1/2 cup shredded cheddar cheese

In a large skillet, brown ground beef, drain grease. Add taco seasoning, prepare according to package. In a muffin tin, press biscuits on bottom and up sides of muffin cups. Fill each biscuit with ground beef. Bake for 15 minutes. Sprinkle with cheese. Bake for 3 minutes or until cheese is melted.

Makes 10 cups   Mild

In 1912 a method was developed by Wilbur Scoville to rate the heat in peppers. A pepper's heat is rated in Scoville Units. A Bell Pepper rates a zero, while a Habanero Pepper can rate over 350,000 Scoville Units.

Armadillo Eggs

Preheat oven to 325 degrees

1 pound sausage
2 cups flour
1 (16 ounce) package cheddar cheese, shredded
1 tablespoon garlic salt
1 tablespoon crushed red pepper
24 Jalapeno peppers
1 (16 ounce) package Monterey Jack cheese, cubed

In a medium bowl, combine sausage, flour, chedder cheese, garlic salt, and red pepper. Slit each Jalapeno down the center, remove seeds. Stuff each Jalapeno with Monterey Jack cheese cubes. Shape sausage mixture around each Jalapeno pepper. Place on a lightly greased 9 x 13 inch baking pan. Bake for 30 minutes or until golden brown.

Makes 12 servings   Wild & Hot

 Scoville Units measure the amount of capsaicin in the pepper and the number of units of water it takes to neutralize the heat. Capsaicin is an oil found in peppers and is what makes a pepper hot.

Mini Mexi Bowls

Preheat oven to 425 degrees

4 (12 inch) flour tortillas
3 ounces white cheddar cheese, shredded
1/3 cup black beans, rinsed and drained
1 cup green bell pepper, chopped
3 ounces Monterey Jack cheese, shredded
1 tomato, diced
2 tablespoons diced onion
3 ounces cheddar cheese, shredded
2 tablespoons salsa

Cut each tortilla into 4 wedges. Place them into lightly greased muffin tins. Layer ingredients evenly in each tortilla as they appear in recipe. Bake for 10 minutes or until lightly browned.

Makes 28 servings   Mild

Chile Squares

Preheat oven to 350 degrees

3 (4 ounce) cans chopped green chiles
3 eggs, lightly beaten
2 cups shredded cheddar cheese

In a greased 8 x 8 inch pan, spread green chiles evenly. Pour eggs gently over green chiles. Sprinkle top with cheese. Bake for 20 to 25 minutes or until cheese is melted. Cool and cut into squares. Serve on crackers or eat alone.

Makes 3 Dozen   Mild

When refrigerating recipes containing hot peppers, your leftover will become spicier as the peppers continue to release their heat.

Jalapeno Squares

Preheat oven to 350 degrees

1 cup evaporated milk
3/4 cup water
3 eggs, beaten
1/4 cup butter or margarine, melted
1 cup flour
1 teaspoon baking powder
2 cups shredded cheddar cheese
1/4 cup chopped green onions
4 Jalapeno peppers, seeded and
  chopped

In a medium bowl, combine milk, water, eggs, and butter. Add flour and baking powder, mix well. Add cheese, onions and Jalapeno, mix. Spread mixture evenly into a lightly greased 9 x 13 inch baking dish. Bake for 30 minutes or until lightly browned. Cool and cut into squares.

Makes 24 - 1 Inch servings   Wild & Hot

Mild Version: *Exchange the Jalapeno peppers for 1 (4 ounce) can of diced green chiles.*

 Some chile peppers can grow up to 12 inches long or as short as 1/4 inch.

Cheesy Chile Squares

Preheat oven to 350 degrees

4 eggs, beaten
1/4 cup flour
1 tablespoon butter, melted
1/2 teaspoon baking powder
1/2 teaspoon salt
1/4 teaspoon pepper
1 cup cottage cheese
1 cup shredded cheddar cheese
1 cup shredded Monterey Jack cheese
2 (4 ounce) cans diced green chiles

In a medium size bowl, combine eggs, flour, butter, baking powder, salt, and pepper. Add all cheeses and chiles, stir well. Pour mixture into a lightly greased 8 x 8 inch baking dish. Bake for 30 to 35 minutes.

Makes 8 servings   Medium

Mild Chile Peppers: Anaheim, Pablano, and Ancho Peppers.

Salsa Bites

Preheat oven to 400 degrees

4 eggs
1 1/2 cups shredded cheddar cheese
1/2 cup salsa
1/4 cup flour
2 tablespoons diced green onion
2 teaspoons chili powder

In a medium bowl, combine all ingredients. Mix well. In a lightly greased muffin pan, spoon 1 tablespoon of egg mixture. Bake for 10 minutes or until golden brown. Serve warm.

Makes 24 servings   Medium

Cheese Snack

Preheat oven to 350 degrees

**1 (16 ounce) package shredded
mozzarella cheese**
**1 (16 ounce) package shredded
cheddar cheese**
4 eggs beaten
1 (16 ounce) jar salsa

In a medium size bowl, combine mozzarella cheese, cheddar cheese, and eggs. Pour mixture into a lightly oiled 9 x 13 inch baking dish. Top with salsa. Bake for 40 minutes. Let stand for 5 minutes before cutting into squares. Serve with crackers or tortilla chips.

Makes 24 servings   Mild

 Medium Chile Peppers: Cascabel, Chilaca, Pasilla, Chiptole, and Jalapeno Peppers.

Santa Fe Deviled Eggs

12 hard boiled eggs
**1 (4 ounce) can chopped green chiles,
drained**
2/3 cup sour cream
**2 tablespoons mustard
paprika**

Slice eggs in half lengthwise. Place egg yolks in a medium bowl and mash, stir in remaining ingredients. Mix well, spoon about 1 rounded tablespoon of the egg mixture into each egg white half. Garnish with paprika.

Makes 24 servings   Medium

Taco Wings

Preheat oven to 375 degrees

12 chicken wings
1 (1.25 ounce) taco seasoning

Coat chicken wings with taco seasoning, place on a lightly greased 9 x 13 inch baking dish. Bake for 40 minutes or until no longer pink. Serve with salsa.

Makes 6 servings   Medium

Hot Chile Peppers: Cayenne, Serrano, and Pequin Peppers.

Ball Of Fire

2 (8 ounce) packages cream cheese, softened
1/4 cup shredded pepper jack cheese
3/4 cup shredded cheddar cheese
1/2 green bell pepper, minced
1 teaspoon Worcestershire sauce
1 Jalapeno pepper, minced
1/2 teaspoon garlic salt
3/4 cup chopped cilantro

In a medium bowl combine all ingredients except the cilantro. Mix well and form the mixture into a ball. Roll the ball in the chopped cilantro, or if you prefer it may be rolled in parsley or shredded cheese. Serve with your favorite cracker.

Makes 12 servings   Wild & Hot

Mild Version: Remove seeds from the Jalapeno pepper and use mozzarella cheese instead of the pepper jack cheese.

Sweet and Spicy Wings

Preheat oven to 400 degrees

1 cup salsa
1/4 cup honey
1/2 teaspoon chili powder
12 chicken wings

In a small bowl, combine salsa, honey, and chili powder. Dip wings into salsa mixture and place on a lightly greased baking sheet. Bake for 50 minutes or until no longer pink. Brush with sauce during baking.

Makes 12 servings   Medium

Spicy Shrimp Tortillas

Preheat broiler

1 tablespoon ground cumin
2 teaspoons chili powder
1 teaspoon salt
1 teaspoon garlic salt
1/2 teaspoon Cayenne pepper
1 pound medium size shrimp
1 cup guacamole
36 tortilla chips

In a small bowl, combine cumin, chili powder, salt, garlic salt, and Cayenne pepper. Sprinkle the shrimp with spice mixture. Place shrimp on a lightly greased broiler pan. Broil for 4 minutes or until cooked through. Top each chip with guacamole, place shrimp on guacamole and serve.

Make 36 servings   Medium

Extremely Hot Chile Peppers: Habanero and Scotch Bonnet Peppers.

Southwestern Veggie Quesadillas

4 (12 inch) flour tortilla
3/4 cup shredded cheddar cheese
1/2 cup diced red bell pepper
1/2 cup corn, drained
1/2 cup black beans, drained
1 chopped green onion

Quesadillas are a popular item sold by street venders in Mexico.

In a lightly oiled skillet over medium heat place one tortilla, flipping it to heat both sides, set aside and repeat. After heating a second tortilla, begin at the center and spread the cheese evenly to cover entire surface of tortilla. Top the cheese with vegetables; place precooked tortilla on top to make a sandwich. Cover with a lid, heat until the cheese is melted, remove and cut into 4 wedges each. Serve warm

Makes 16 wedges   Mild

Burrito Quesadillas

Preheat oven to 400 degrees

12 (8 inch) flour tortillas
1 (16 ounce) can refried beans
1 cup shredded Monterey Jack cheese
1/2 cup salsa
1/4 cup chopped with tops, green onions

Place 6 tortillas on baking sheets. Layer equal amounts of refried beans, cheese, salsa, and onion. Top with remaining tortillas. Bake for 10 minutes. Cut into 4 wedges each and serve.

Makes 24 servings   Mild

Olive Poppers

Preheat oven to 400 degrees

24 green olives
1 cup shredded cheddar cheese
2 tablespoons butter or margarine,
softened
1 tablespoon water
1/2 cup flour
1/4 teaspoon Cayenne pepper

Drain olives and pat dry. In a small bowl combine cheese, butter, and water. Add flour and Cayenne pepper, mix well. Mold a teaspoon size ball of dough around each olive, place on a lightly greased baking sheet. Bake for 15 minutes or until golden brown. Serve warm.

Makes 12 servings   Medium

Mild Version: Use garlic powder in place of the Cayenne pepper.

Chile Cheese Loaf

1 (2 pound) block Velveeta® cheese,
room temperature
1 (8 ounce) package cream cheese,
softened
1 (12 ounce) can diced green chiles
1 (8 ounce) can diced black olives

Place Velveeta® cheese block on a serving platter. Spread cream cheese on top of the processed cheese. In a small bowl mix the green chiles and black olives, spread on top of cream cheese. Serve with crackers.

Makes 32 servings   Mild

 Salsa: For a sweet and spicy flavor, exchange fresh pitted cherries for tomatoes in your favorite salsa recipe.

Chile Spirals

8 (8 inch) soft tortilla taco shells
1 (8 ounces) package cream cheese,
   softened
2 (4 ounce) cans diced green chiles
6 green onions, sliced
1 red pepper, diced
2 (2.25 ounce) cans chopped black
   olives, drained

In a medium size bowl, combine all ingredients, except tortilla shells, mix well. Spread 1/2 cup of cheese mixture over each tortilla, roll up tortilla. Wrap each roll in plastic wrap; refrigerate for 1 hour. Remove plastic wrap and slice into 1 inch rolls.

Makes 24 servings   Mild

Quick Tip: Soften cream cheese by removing foil wrapper and microwave for 30 to 45 seconds.

Jalapeno Rice Cakes

Preheat oven to 400 degrees

4 rice cakes
1/4 cup refried beans
1/4 cup salsa
1 cup shredded cheddar cheese
1/4 cup sliced Jalapeno peppers

Spread beans on each rice cake, place on baking sheet. Spread salsa over beans. Sprinkle cheese over salsa. Top with Jalapeno peppers. Bake 10 minutes.

Makes 4 servings   Wild & Hot

Mild Version: Use mild salsa or fresh chopped tomato. Eliminate Jalapeno peppers. Use mild chopped green chiles instead of Jalapeno peppers.

Throw Caution to the Wind

Sauces, Soups & Salads

Enchilada Sauce

2 tablespoons vegetable oil
2 tablespoons flour
2 tablespoons chili powder
2 cups water
1 (8 ounce) can tomato sauce
1 teaspoon salt
1/2 teaspoon ground cumin
1/4 teaspoon garlic powder

In a large saucepan, heat oil over medium heat. Stir in flour and chili powder; cook 1 minute. Add remaining ingredients. Bring to a boil. Reduce heat; simmer 10 minutes.

Makes 3 cups   Medium

Red Chile

8 dried red chile peppers, seeded
4 cups water
2 tablespoons flour
2 tablespoons vegetable oil
1/2 teaspoon dried oregano
1 teaspoon white wine vinegar

In a large saucepan, combine chile peppers and water, bring to a boil. Boil 5 minutes. Set aside to cool 15 minutes. Place chile peppers and water in blender; cover and blend well. Pass chile mixture through a strainer, pressing with a wooden spoon. In a medium skillet, sauté flour in oil over medium heat for 2 minutes. Add chile mixture, garlic, oregano, and vinegar. Mix well. Simmer 20 minutes.

Make 6 servings   Medium

Flour tortillas are not considered Mexican food. Tortillas are traditionally made of corn.

Chile Chicken Soup

1 (3 1/2 pounds) chicken
3 quarts water
2 teaspoons salt
2 bay leaves
1 cup chopped celery
1 onion, chopped
1 tomato, chopped
1 (4 ounce) can diced green chiles
2 (7/8 ounce) envelopes chicken gravy mix
2 teaspoons Worcestershire sauce
1/4 teaspoon pepper
1/8 teaspoon ground thyme
2 cups extra wide egg noodles, uncooked

In a large soup pot, place chicken, water, salt and bay leaves. Cover and simmer for 1 hour or until tender. Remove bay leaves, skin, and bones from chicken. Cut chicken into bite size pieces, return to broth. Add celery, onion, tomato, green chiles, gravy mix, Worcestershire, pepper, and thyme. Bring to a boil. Add noodles; simmer for 10 to 15 minutes or until tender.

Makes 8 servings   Mild

Easy Tortilla Soup

1 (49 1/2 ounce) can chicken broth
1 (14 1/2 ounce) can black beans, drained
1 (14 1/4 ounce) sweet corn, drained
1 (16 ounce) jar salsa
3 cups tortilla chips
1 1/2 cups shredded cheddar cheese

In a large saucepan, combine chicken broth, black beans, corn, and salsa. Simmer for 15 minutes. Place tortilla chips into bowls. Ladle soup over tortilla chips and top with cheddar cheese.

Makes 6 servings   Mild

How to Peel Peppers: Place Jalapenos on a broiler pan. Place pan 4 inches from heat until skin blisters, about 2 minutes. Rotate 1/4 turn and broil, repeat until all sides are blistered.

(continued →)

58

Tortilla Soup

1 clove garlic, minced
2 tablespoons vegetable oil
1/2 onion, chopped
4 cups chicken broth
1/2 red bell pepper, chopped
3/4 teaspoon Basil leaves
1 tablespoon ground red pepper
1/4 teaspoon black pepper
1/2 teaspoon salt
1 (15 ounce) can tomato puree
2 cups cooked and cubed chicken breast
10 - 6 inch corn tortillas,
    cut into 1/2 inch strips
1/2 cup vegetable oil
2 cups cheddar cheese

In a large soup pot, brown the garlic and onion in 2 tablespoons of oil. Stir in chicken broth, bell pepper, Basil leaves, red pepper, black pepper, salt, tomato puree, and chicken. Heat to boiling. Reduce heat, and simmer uncovered for 30 minutes. In a skillet heat 1/2 cup oil until hot. Cook tortilla strips in oil until light golden brown, place on a paper towel to drain. Divide tortilla strips in bowls. Pour soup over strips and top with cheddar cheese.

Makes 6 servings   Medium

Place immediately in a brown paper bag, close and let stand for 20 minutes. Using plastic gloves, peel off charred skin. Remove stems and seeds.

Posole

1 tablespoon vegetable oil
1 large onion, chopped
4 cloves garlic, minced
1 pound boneless pork loin, cubed
2 (15 ounce) hominy, drained
1 (15 ounce) can tomato sauce
1 1/2 cups chicken broth
2 tablespoons chili powder
1 teaspoon dried oregano, crushed
1/4 cup chicken broth
2 tablespoons flour

In a large saucepan, heat oil over medium high heat. Add onion and garlic; sauté until tender. Add pork; cook until lightly browned. Stir in hominy, tomato sauce, 1 1/2 cups chicken broth, chili powder, and oregano. Bring to a boil. Reduce heat, cover and simmer 15 minutes. In a small bowl, combine 1/4 cup chicken broth and flour. Add to saucepan. Mix well. Cook uncovered over medium heat until soup thickens.

Makes 4 servings   Medium

Tex-Mex is a combination of food from Texas and Mexico. Some times referred to as American style Mexican food.

Pancho Polo Soup

1 pound chicken breast,
  boneless and skinless
5 carrots, chopped
3 celery stalks, chopped
2 potatoes, cubed
1 green pepper, chopped
1 (14 1/2 ounce) can tomatoes,
  undrained
2 (4 ounce) cans mushrooms, drained
2 chicken bouillon cubes
2 teaspoons sugar
1 1/2 teaspoons chili powder
1 teaspoon Cayenne pepper
1/4 teaspoon pepper
1 tablespoon cornstarch
2 cups water

In a 5 quart slow cooker, combine all
ingredients except the cornstarch and
water, mix well. In a small bowl, combine
cornstarch and water, mix until smooth.
Stir cornstarch mixture into the slow cooker,
mix well. Cover and cook on low for 8 -10
hours or until vegetables are tender.

Makes 6 servings   Medium

Mild Version: *Eliminate the Cayenne pepper,*
and reduce the chili powder to 1/2 teaspoon.

Picante
means hot
to the
taste buds.

Enchilada Soup

1¹/₂ cups chicken broth
10 (6 inch) corn tortillas, cut into
   ¹/₂ inch strips
1 Jalapeno pepper, seeded and chopped
1 teaspoon cumin
1 (10 ounce) can red enchilada sauce
1 cup green enchilada sauce
4 chicken breasts, cooked and cut into
   bite size pieces
1 cup half and half
1 cup shredded cheddar cheese
1 tomato, chopped

In a large saucepan over medium heat, combine chicken broth, tortillas, Jalapeno pepper, and cumin. Simmer for 15 minutes. Add enchilada sauces, chicken, and half-and-half. Heat then ladle into bowls. Top with cheese and tomatoes and serve.

Makes 6 servings   Wild & Hot

Mild Version: Use a 4 ounce can of tomato paste and ¹/₂ cup of water instead of red enchilada sauce. Eliminate the Jalapeno pepper.

If your soup is too salty, add a raw cut potato. Discard after they have cooked.

Taco Soup

1 pound hamburger
1/2 cup chopped onion
2 (16 ounce) cans stewed tomatoes
2 (16 ounce) cans kidney beans
3 cups water
4 teaspoons taco seasoning mix
2 (8 ounce) cans tomato sauce

In a large soup pot, brown hamburger and onion. Drain grease. Combine remaining ingredients (undrained). Add to hamburger; simmer 25 minutes.

Serves 8.   Mild

Serving Suggestion: top each serving with crushed tortilla chips, shredded cheddar cheese and a dollop of sour cream

Amigo Beef Soup

1 pound ground beef
2 cloves garlic, minced
1 onion, chopped
2 potatoes, diced
1 (15 ounce) can pinto beans, rinsed
    and drained
1 (15 ounce) can Mexican style stewed
    tomatoes, diced
3 (4 ounce) cans chopped green chiles
2 cups water
1 teaspoon salt
1/2 teaspoon black pepper

In a large soup pot, brown ground beef, garlic, and onion. Drain grease. Add potatoes, beans, stewed tomatoes, green chiles, water, salt and pepper. Bring to a boil. Reduce and simmer covered for 45 minutes or until potato is tender.

Makes 8 servings   Medium

Cinco de Mayo — May 5th celebrates the Mexican Army's victory over the French Army in 1862 at the Battle of Puebla.

Carne Soup

1 pound stew beef
1/2 head cabbage, chopped
4 Jalapeno peppers, seeded and chopped
3 potatoes, cubed
3 carrots, sliced
1 tomato, chopped
1 onion, chopped
4 teaspoons minced cilantro
4 cloves minced garlic
1 teaspoon salt
1/2 teaspoon pepper
1/4 teaspoon ground cumin
2 tablespoons fresh lime juice

In a large soup pot, over medium heat, brown beef. Add cabbage, Jalapeno peppers, potatoes, carrots, tomato, onion, cilantro, garlic, salt, pepper, and cumin. Add water to cover ingredients, stir well. Bring to a boil. Reduce heat, cover and simmer 2 hours. Stir in lime juice just before serving

Makes 6 servings   Wild & Hot

Mild Version: Eliminate Jalapeno peppers. Add one 4 ounce can mild green chiles, chopped.

Beans and corn when put together provide a full supply of amino acids, the building blocks of protein.

Mexican Meatball Soup

1/2 cup chopped onion
1 clove garlic, minced
2 tablespoons vegetable oil
2 (10 1/2 ounce) cans beef broth
4 cups water
1 (6 ounce) can tomato paste
2 cups cubed potato
1 cup sliced carrots
1 egg
1/4 cup rice, uncooked
1/4 cup cilantro
1 teaspoon salt
1/2 teaspoon oregano
1/4 teaspoon pepper
1 pound lean ground beef

In a large soup pot, over medium high heat, sauté onion and garlic in vegetable oil till onion is transparent. Add broth, water, and tomato paste, bring to a boil. Reduce heat, add potatoes and carrots, and simmer for 5 minutes. In a medium bowl, combine egg, rice, cilantro, salt, oregano, and pepper, mix well. Add ground beef to egg mixture, mix well. Form beef into 1 inch balls, add to soup one at a time. Return soup to a boil then reduce and simmer 45 minutes or until meat balls and vegetables are fully cooked.

Makes 10 servings   Mild

Refrigerate leftover beans for up to 5 days. They make a nice addition to salads and soups.

Flaming Pilgrim Soup

1 pound ground turkey
2 (14.5 ounce) cans chicken broth
1 (16 ounce) can chili beans, undrained
1 (11 ounce) can Mexican style corn, drained
1 (16 ounce) jar thick and chunky salsa
1 teaspoon salt
1/4 teaspoon pepper
3 tablespoons fresh minced cilantro
1/2 cup sour cream
2 tablespoons guacamole

In a large soup pot, over medium high heat, brown ground turkey. Add chicken broth, chili beans, corn, salsa, salt, and pepper. Bring to a boil. Reduce heat, cover and simmer 20 minutes. Stir in cilantro; simmer an additional 10 minutes. In a small bowl, combine sour cream and guacamole. Ladle soup into bowls and top with sour cream mixture.

Makes 6 servings   Mild

Cilantro, you either love it or hate it. People who love it say it has a citrus flavor and those who hate say it has a soapy flavor.

Old West Ham + Bean Soup

1 pound brown beans
1 Jalapeno pepper, seeded, diced
1 teaspoon salt
1 cup diced ham

In a large bowl, cover beans with water; soak over night. Drain water from beans and transfer to large soup pot; cover with clean water. Add Jalapeno pepper and salt. Bring to a boil. Reduce heat, cover and simmer 1 hour. Stir in ham; simmer an additional 30 minutes.

Makes 6 Servings   Medium

Mild Version: Eliminate Jalapeno peppers. Use 1 fresh green chile, seeded and chopped.

Spicy Bean + Ham Soup

1/2 pound hot Italian sausage, casings
   removed and crumbled
1 cup chopped onions
2 teaspoons minced garlic
1/4 pound ham, diced
5 cups chicken broth
1 (15 1/2 ounce) can garbanzo beans,
   undrained
2 (15 ounce) cans navy beans, undrained
1 (10 ounce) can tomatoes and green
   chiles, chopped
1 teaspoon cumin
2 cups unpeeled and diced potatoes
1 (10 ounce) package frozen spinach,
   thawed

In a large soup pot, brown sausage and
onion, drain grease. Add garlic, stir 1 minute.
Add ham, cook 3 minutes. Stir in chicken
broth, garbanzo beans, navy beans, tomatoes
and chiles, and potatoes. Heat until it boils,
reduce heat and simmer 20 minutes. Stir in
thawed spinach, simmer 10 minutes.

Makes 8 Servings   Wild & Hot

*Mild Version: Use mild Italian sausage and
eliminate the cumin. Use stewed tomatoes in the
place of tomatoes and green chiles.*

 Just like
parsley,
   cilantro
can help settle
your stomach.
Some people
also call
cilantro,
coriander.

New Mexico Bean Soup

1 pound pork sausage
3 cloves garlic, minced
1/4 cup chopped onion
1 teaspoon salt
1/2 teaspoon pepper
3 (10 3/4 ounce) cans chicken broth
2 potatoes, cubed
4 carrots, sliced
1 (10 1/2 ounce) can chili beans, drained
1 (10 1/2 ounce) can black beans,
   drained and rinsed
1 (10 1/2 ounce) can pinto beans,
   rinsed and drained
1 (15 ounce) can corn, drained
1 cup salsa
1/2 cup chopped cilantro

In a large soup pot, over medium high heat, brown sausage, garlic, onion, salt, and pepper. Drain grease. Add chicken broth, potatoes, and carrots. Bring to a boil, reduce heat and simmer covered for 45 minutes. Stir in chili beans, black beans, pinto beans, corn, salsa, and cilantro. Simmer 20 minutes.

Makes 8 servings   Mild

In Mexican cooking, cilantro is the most popular herb.

Refried Bean Soup

3 cups tomato juice
1 (16 ounce) jar thick and chunky salsa
1 (16 ounce) can refried beans
1 (1.25 ounce) package taco seasoning
1 cup water
2 cups shredded cheddar cheese, divided
2 cups corn chips, crushed

In a large saucepan, combine tomato juice, salsa, refried beans, taco seasoning, water, 1 cup cheese. Bring to a boil. Reduce heat and simmer for 20 minutes. Top each serving with remaining cheese and corn chips.

Makes 6 servings   Mild

Cilantro was once thought to be an aphrodisiac.

Fiery Fish Soup

2 Jalapeno peppers, seeded
2 tomatoes, quartered
2 tablespoons cilantro
1 onion, quartered
1 clove garlic, crushed
2 pounds fillet of Sole
1/2 cup water
1/3 cup olive oil
3 tablespoons lemon juice
1/2 teaspoon salt

In a blender puree Jalapeno peppers, tomatoes, cilantro, onion, and garlic. Place fish in a large saucepan, add vegetable puree. Stir in water, olive oil, lemon juice, and salt. Cover and simmer 20 minutes. Serve with rice.

Makes 6 servings   Wild & Hot

Mild Version: Eliminate Jalapeno pepper. Use a mild green chile.

Pescado Soup

1 tablespoon vegetable oil
1/2 cup chopped green pepper
1/4 cup chopped onion
1 clove garlic, minced
1 1/2 cups chicken broth
1 tablespoon chili powder
1 teaspoon ground cumin
1/2 teaspoon salt
1 (4 ounce) can green chiles
1 1/2 cups diced canned tomatoes
4 drops hot pepper sauce
1 cup shrimp
1/2 pound cod fillets
3/4 cup sour cream

Add oil to a large soup pot, combine green pepper, onion and garlic over medium high heat and sauté until onion is tender. Add chicken broth, chili powder, cumin, and salt. Bring to a boil, reduce heat and simmer 20 minutes. Add green chiles, tomatoes, hot pepper sauce, shrimp, and cod. Return to boil, reduce heat and simmer 5 minutes. Stir in sour cream and serve.

Makes 4 servings   Medium

If your soup has too much garlic in it, place parsley flakes in a cheesecloth bag and add to the pot until it soaks up the excess garlic.

Pachuca Pumpkin Soup

1 pound ground turkey
1 cup chopped red bell pepper
1/2 cup chopped onion
1 clove garlic
1 (15 ounce) can pumpkin
2 (14.5 ounce) cans tomatoes
   with juice, diced
1 (15 ounce) can tomato sauce
1 (15.25) can kidney beans, drained
1 (4 ounce) can green chiles, diced
1/2 cup canned corn, drained
1 tablespoon chili powder
1 teaspoon ground cumin
1/2 teaspoon salt

In a large soup pot, over medium high heat brown turkey, bell pepper, onion, and garlic. Drain. Add remaining ingredients, bring to a boil, reduce heat. Simmer for 30 minutes.

Makes 4 servings.   Mild

Most types of soup freeze well. Except soups containing cheese, cream, or other dairy products.

Correcto Corn Potato Soup

1 tablespoon olive oil
1/4 cup chopped red pepper
1/2 cup chopped onion
1/4 cup chopped celery
1 (14 1/2 ounce) can chicken broth
2 cups diced potato
3 cups milk
2 (15 1/4 ounce) cans whole kernel corn
1 (4 ounce) can green chiles
1/2 cup shredded cheddar cheese

In a large sauce pan over medium high heat, add oil, pepper, onion, celery, cook until tender. Add broth and potatoes, bring to a boil. Reduce heat, cover and simmer 10 minutes or until potatoes are tender. Add milk, corn, green chiles, and cheese, simmer 5 minutes

Makes 6 Servings   Medium

The Spaniards named the corn based flat bread they found in Mexico, tortillas.

Green Chile

3 pounds boneless pork shoulder,
   cut in 1/2 inch pieces
2 tablespoons vegetable oil
1 clove garlic, minced
1 (28 ounce) can tomatoes, chopped
5 green chiles, seeded and chopped
2 teaspoons ground cumin
1/2 teaspoon sugar
1/2 teaspoon salt

In a large skillet, brown pork in oil, cook on both sides, remove and set aside. Sauté the garlic in the same pan. In a large soup pot, add tomatoes and liquid, green chiles, and seasoning, bring to a boil, reduce and simmer. Add meat and garlic with the oil. Cover and simmer for 1 hour.

Makes 8 Servings   Medium

Green Chile Soup

2 tablespoons butter
2 cups chopped onion
1 clove garlic, minced
2 bay leaves
1/2 teaspoon oregano
31/2 cups chicken broth
1 pound potatoes, peeled and diced
1/4 teaspoon black pepper
1/2 teaspoon salt
1 (8 ounce) can diced green chiles
1/3 cup whipping cream
2 cups shredded Monterey Jack cheese

Melt butter in a 4 quart saucepan. Add onions, garlic, bay leaves, and oregano, sauté for 5 minutes. Stir in chicken broth, potatoes, pepper, and salt. Bring to a boil, reduce heat and simmer for 25 minutes or until potatoes are tender. Cool soup slightly, discarding bay leaves. Puree soup in a food processor or blender. Return soup to pan, stir in green chiles, heat over medium heat, simmer 15 minutes. Stir in cream. Ladle soup into bowls and top with Monterey Jack cheese.

Makes 6 servings   Mild

Mild Version: Use 4 ounces of mild green chiles.

When Columbus first discovered the chile pepper he believed it to be a new type of black pepper.

Green Chile Stew

1 cup chopped onion
3 cloves garlic, minced
3 tablespoons vegetable oil
3 pounds pork tenderloin, cut in bite
  size pieces
1/4 cup flour
3/4 cup chicken broth
2 (14.5 ounce) cans tomatoes, chopped
2 (7 ounce) cans green chiles, chopped
1 teaspoon salt

In a large soup pot, over medium high heat, sauté onion and garlic in vegetable oil until onion is tender. Add pork and flour, cook until pork is fully cooked. Stir in broth, tomatoes, green chiles, and salt. Bring to a boil. Reduce heat, cover and simmer 25 minutes.

Makes 8 servings   Medium

Mild Version: Eliminate the 2 (7 ounce) cans of green chiles. Add one 4 ounce can green chiles, chopped.

To keep chiles fresh, wrap them in a paper towel and place in a paper sack and refrigerate. They can be stored up to two weeks and still keep their fresh taste.

Chile Verde Con Queso

3 potatoes, diced
1 onion, diced
1 carrot, thinly sliced
1/4 cup vegetable oil
3 cups chicken broth
1 cup water
1 cup nonfat dry milk
1/4 cup flour
6 green chile peppers, chopped
1 (8 ounce) package Monterey Jack
  cheese

In a large soup pot, sauté potatoes, onion, and carrot in vegetable oil until onions are transparent. Add chicken broth, cover and simmer for 45 minutes or until tender. Combine water, dry milk, and flour, mix until smooth. Add flour mixture to broth, stir until blended. Add green chile peppers and cheese, stir until cheese is melted. Simmer 5 minutes, do not boil.

Makes 8 servings   Wild & Hot

Mild Version: Reduce chile peppers to 1. Remove seeds.

Dried chiles should be stored in a cool, dry place or frozen in freezer bags.

Cream of Chile Soup

1/4 cup butter or margarine
2 cups chopped onion
2 bay leaves
1 clove garlic, minced
1/2 teaspoon oregano
3 1/2 cups chicken broth
3 (4 ounce) cans diced green chiles
3 potatoes, peeled and diced
1/2 teaspoon salt
1/4 teaspoon black pepper
1/4 teaspoon ground cumin
1/3 cup heavy whipping cream
2 (6 inch) corn tortillas
2 cups shredded Monterey Jack cheese

In a large soup pot, over medium low heat, sauté butter, onion, bay leaves, garlic, and oregano. Sauté until onions are tender. Add chicken broth, green chiles, potatoes, salt, pepper, and cumin. Bring to a boil, reduce heat and simmer for 30 minutes. Stir in cream. In a large skillet over medium high heat, heat corn tortillas until they are crisp. Cut into 1/2 inch strips. Ladle soup into bowls. Top with Monterey Jack cheese and tortilla strips.

Makes 6 servings   Mild

The pepper that is most often added to salads or stuffed is the Anaheim pepper.

Hot Potato Soup

1 pound bacon
5 medium sized potatoes, diced
1 (10 ounce) can evaporated milk
6 cups water
2 tablespoons butter
2 tablespoons flour
4 Jalapeno peppers, seeded
   and deveined
2 Serranos peppers, seeded
   and deveined
1/2 teaspoon salt
1/4 teaspoon black peeper
2 large onions, diced
4 celery stalks, diced

In a large skillet cook bacon until well done, drain bacon on a paper towel. In a large soup pot, boil potatoes until firm not mushy. Drain water, crumble bacon and add to potatoes along with evaporated milk, water, butter and flour. In a blender, puree Jalapeno and Serena peppers. Add to soup, heat over medium heat for 30 minutes. Add diced onions and celery; cook for an additional 10 minutes.

Makes 10 servings   Wild & Hot

Mild Version: *Eliminate peppers, use a 4-ounce can of mild peppers in its place.*

 The first cook book featuring a recipe using peppers was published in 1872.

Mexican Onion Soup

3 cups sliced onion
$1/4$ teaspoon garlic powder
3 tablespoons butter or margarine
$2 1/2$ cups tomato juice
1 ($14 1/2$ ounce) can beef broth
$1/2$ cup salsa
$1/2$ teaspoon salt
1 cup Italian flavored croutons
1 cup shredded Monterey Jack cheese

In a large saucepan over medium high heat, brown onion and garlic powder in butter until golden. Add tomato juice, broth, salsa, and salt, bring to a boil. Reduce heat, cover and simmer 10 minutes. Ladle soup into 6 bowls. Sprinkle croutons then cheese into each bowl and serve.

Makes 6 servings   Mild

The first cook book using tomatoes was published in 1692

Rapido Rice Soup

3 cups chicken broth
$1/2$ cup white rice, uncooked
$1/4$ cup salsa
1 teaspoon salt

In a large saucepan combine all ingredients. Cover, simmer 20 minutes or until rice is tender.

Makes 4 servings   Mild

Aztec Corn Chowder

2 tablespoons butter

1½ cups chopped onion

1 teaspoon chili powder

1 teaspoon cumin

1 tablespoon flour

1 (16 ounce) package frozen corn, thawed

1 (14½ ounce) can chicken broth

2 cups salsa

1 (8 ounce) package cream cheese

In a large saucepan brown onions in butter. Stir in chili powder, cumin, and flour. Add corn, chicken broth, and salsa, bring to a boil. In a small bowl add ½ cup soup mixture to the cream cheese, mix until blended. Stir cream cheese mixture into soup. Simmer 15 minutes.

Makes 6 servings   Medium

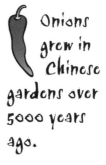

Onions grew in Chinese gardens over 5000 years ago.

Zuni Zucchini Soup

5 potatoes, diced
2 cups chicken broth
2 onions, diced
1 tablespoon butter
5 medium zucchini, peeled and chopped
1 teaspoons chili powder
1/2 teaspoon salt
1/4 teaspoon pepper
1 cup sour cream

In a large soup pot, over medium high heat, simmer potatoes in chicken broth. In a large skillet, add butter and onions; sauté over medium high heat until onions are transparent. Add the onions and the zucchini to chicken broth, cook until tender. Add seasonings and sour cream, heat and serve.

Makes 3 servings   Mild

In Egypt onions were worshiped. They believed it symbolized eternity.

Mexican Cabbage Soup

2 pounds lean ground beef
1 onion, chopped
1 small head of cabbage, chopped
1 (10 3/4 ounces) can cream of chicken soup
1 (10 3/4 ounce) can cream of mushroom soup
1 (10 3/4 ounce) can cheddar cheese soup
1 (10 ounce) can tomato and green chiles, chopped
3 cups water

In a large saucepan brown ground beef and onion. Add remaining ingredients. Cover, simmer over medium low heat for 2 hours

Makes 10 servings   Medium

Mild Version: Use a 10 ounce can of stewed tomatoes instead of the can of tomato and green chiles.

Nacho Cheese Soup

1 pound lean ground beef
1/2 cup chopped onion
1 (1.25 ounce) package taco seasoning
2 (10 3/4 ounce) cans cheddar cheese soup
1 cup water
2 cups milk
1/2 cup hot salsa

In a skillet brown ground beef and onion, drain off grease. Add taco seasoning to beef and onions; prepare according to directions on package. In a large saucepan add soup, water, salsa, and meat mixture. Simmer 20 minutes

Makes 8 servings   Medium

Mild Version: Use mild salsa instead of hot salsa and only 1/2 of the package of taco seasoning.

Chipotle Pepper Soup

2 large tomatoes, quartered
1 onion, quartered
1 cup chopped fresh cilantro
4 cups chicken broth
1 Chipotle pepper, chopped
1 1/2 teaspoons salt
2 avocados, peeled, pitted, and diced
3 cups tortilla chips

In a blender, puree tomatoes, onion, and cilantro. In a large soup pot, combine chicken broth, Chiptole pepper, salt, and pureed vegetables. Bring to a boil. Reduce heat, cover and simmer 20 minutes. Ladle soup into bowls. Top with avocado and tortilla chips.

Makes 6 servings   Mild

 Pilgrims brought onions with them on the Mayflower. When they arrived in America, they found wild onions growing.

Gazpacho

3 cups tomato juice
3 onions, chopped
1/2 cup olive oil
3 tablespoons red wine vinegar
3 garlic cloves, minced
1 tablespoon salt
3 mild green peppers, seeded and
  chopped
3 cucumbers, peeled and chopped
3 teaspoons cilantro, minced
14 teaspoons sour cream

In a blender place, tomato juice, onion, olive oil, and vinegar; puree. Add all remaining ingredients, except sour cream, puree until smooth. Chill before serving. Top with a dollop of sour cream before serving.

Makes 12 servings   Mild

Onions are grown primarily in western Idaho and eastern Oregon. 14 other states also grow onions.

White Lighting Chile

3/4 pound ground turkey
2 (14 ounce) cans Great Northern beans,
  drained and rinsed
1 (8 ounce) package cheddar cheese
  with Jalapeno pepper, cubed
1 (14 1/2 ounce) can corn, drained
1 cup hot salsa
1 cup water

In a large soup pot, brown ground turkey, drain all grease. Stir in remaining ingredients. Simmer over low heat for 30 minutes, or until cheese is completely melted.

Makes 8 Servings   Medium

Quick Draw Chile Soup

1 (10 1/2 ounce) can condensed bean
   and bacon soup
1 (10 1/2 ounce) can no bean chili
1 (10 3/4 ounce) can condensed
   tomato soup
1 soup can water

In a large saucepan combine all ingredients.
Simmer on low heat 10 minutes.

Makes 6 Servings   Mild

Inferno Chile

1 1/2 pounds ground beef
1 (16 ounce) can tomatoes,
   chopped with juice
1 (14 1/2 ounce) can beef bullion
12 ounces water
2 cloves garlic, minced
2 medium onions, chopped
4 Jalapeno peppers, chopped
3 tablespoons chili powder
2 teaspoons oregano
1 tablespoon cumin
2 (15 ounce) cans hot chili beans,
   do not drain

In a large soup pot, brown beef, drain
grease. Add all ingredients except the cans of
beans. Cover, simmer for 1 hour. Add beans
and simmer for an additional 15 minutes.

Makes 6 servings   Wild & Hot

 The seeds in peppers taste hot because they are in contact with the veins which are the hottest part of a pepper.

Old El Paso Black Bean Salad

1 (15 1/2 ounce) can black beans,
   drained and rinsed
2 (11 ounce) cans Mexican style corn, drained
1 (4 ounce) can sliced mushrooms, drained
1 large tomato, chopped
2 tablespoons Jalapeno pepper,
   chopped and seeded
1/4 cup chopped onion
3 cloves garlic, minced
1/2 cup cilantro, chopped
1/4 cup olive oil
2 tablespoons red wine vinegar
1/2 teaspoon salt
2 tablespoons lime juice
1 teaspoon chili powder
1 teaspoon cumin

In a large bowl combine, beans, corn, mushrooms tomato, Jalapeno, onion, garlic, and cilantro. Stir Well. In a small bowl, whisk together oil, vinegar, salt, lime juice, chili powder, cumin. Pour over bean mixture and toss gently. Chill 2 hours, serve cold.

Makes 12 servings   Medium

You can actually develop a tolerance to spicy food. Gradually moving from mild to hot foods.

Chile Bean Salad

2 (16 ounce) cans beans in tomato sauce
1 green pepper, chopped
1 onion, chopped
2 tablespoons butter
1 tablespoon chili powder
1/2 teaspoon ground cumin
1/2 teaspoon salt
1/4 teaspoon pepper
1/4 teaspoon oregano
2 drops hot pepper sauce
1/4 cup sour cream
6 lettuce leaves
3 eggs, hard boiled and sliced

Drain and place beans in a large bowl, set aside. In a large skillet over medium high heat, sauté onions and peppers in butter until tender, stir in beans. In a small bowl combine chili powder, cumin, salt, pepper, oregano, hot pepper sauce, and sour cream. Remove bean mixture from heat, add sour cream mixture, toss gently. Place mixture into a bowl, cover and refrigerate. Spoon bean salad onto lettuce leaves, top with egg.

Makes 6 Servings   Mild

Easy Spicy Bean Salad

1 (15 1/2 ounce) can kidney beans
1 (15 1/2 ounce) can garbanzo beans
1 (15 1/2 ounce) can black beans
1 1/2 cups salsa
1 tablespoon red wine vinegar
1 teaspoon celery salt

Drain and rinse all beans, pour into a large bowl. Add salsa, vinegar, and celery salt, mix well. Refrigerate until chilled.

Makes 8 Servings   Mild

The Conquest of Mexico in 1521 by the Spanish captain Cortez and his followers, brought us many culinary delights. Cortez and his followers discovered chocolate, vanilla, beans, peanuts, avocados, coconuts, corn, tomatoes, and squash.

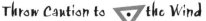

Burrito Salad

1 head lettuce, shredded
1/2 cup chopped green onion
1 1/2 cups ham, diced
1 1/2 cups kidney beans
1 1/4 teaspoons chili powder
1 avocado, sliced
10 (8 inch) flour tortilla shells
Blue Cheese dressing

In a medium bowl, toss lettuce, onion, ham, beans, and chili powder. Place tortillas in individual bowls; fill with lettuce mixture, top with avocado. Top with dressing.

Makes 8 servings   Mild

Tomatoes were once believed to be poisonous.

Santa Cruz Chicken Salsa Salad

1 pound chicken breast,
  boneless and skinless
4 teaspoons taco seasoning mix
1 ripe avocado, peeled and sliced
2 tablespoons lime juice, divided
1 head romaine lettuce, shredded
1 (8 ounce) jar salsa
1 large tomato, chopped
1 large red bell pepper, chopped

Dredge chicken in taco seasoning. In a large skillet over medium high heat, brown chicken. Cut chicken into cubes, set aside to cool. In a small bowl, coat avocado with lime juice. Place lettuce in a large bowl. Spread salsa over lettuce. Sprinkle avocado, tomato,and bell pepper over lettuce. Top with chicken.

Makes 6 servings   Mild

Chama Chicken Salad

2 cups cooked and cubed chicken
1 cup salsa, divided
$1/2$ cup sour cream
4 cups tortilla chips
4 cups shredded lettuce
$1/4$ cup sliced black olives
2 green onions, chopped with tops
$1/2$ cup shredded cheddar cheese

In a small bowl, combine chicken, $1/2$ cup salsa, and sour cream. On a platter, layer chips, lettuce, chicken mixture, olives, onion, cheese, and remaining salsa.

Makes 4 servings.   Mild

Chicken Salsa Salad

2 chicken breasts, cooked and shredded
1 cup salsa
1 head lettuce, shredded
4 teaspoons sour cream

In a small bowl combine chicken and salsa. Place lettuce on 4 plates. Spoon chicken mixture over lettuce. Garnish with sour cream.

Makes 4 servings   Mild

The first tomato plants brought to America were used as decoration in gardens.

Border Town Taco Salad

1 pound ground beef
1/3 cup chopped onion
1 (1.25 ounce) package taco seasoning
2/3 cup water
1 (15 ounce) can kidney beans, drained
1 (8 ounce) package shredded cheddar cheese
1 head lettuce
Thousand Island dressing

In a large skillet, brown hamburger and onion over medium heat. Drain grease from meat. Add taco seasoning and water to hamburger, cook 3 minutes. Cool mixture in the refrigerator. While the meat is cooling, tear lettuce into bite size pieces and place in a large bowl. Add beans, cheese, and meat mixture, toss to mix. Add dressing to taste.

Makes 6 servings   Mild

George Washington Carver encouraged the poor in Alabama to eat tomatoes to enrich their vitamin deficient diets.

Corn Chip Taco Salad

1 pound ground beef
1 (1.25 ounce) package taco seasoning
1 head lettuce, shredded
1 onion, chopped
2 (15 ounce) cans Ranch® beans, drained
1 (16 ounce) package corn chips
1 (8 ounce) bottle French dressing
1 1/2 cups shredded cheddar cheese
2 tomatoes, chopped

In a large skillet over medium high heat, brown ground beef, drain grease. Add package of taco seasoning; prepare according to package directions. Set aside to cool. In a large bowl, combine cooled beef, lettuce, onion, beans, corn chips, and dressing, toss gently to coat. Top with cheese and tomatoes and serve.

Makes 12 servings   Mild

Taco Salad

1 pound ground beef
1 (1.25 ounce) package taco seasoning
1 (15 ounce) cans Ranch® beans, drained
1 head lettuce, shredded
1 cup salsa
1¹/₂ cups shredded cheddar cheese
3 green onions, chopped with tops
1 (2 ounce) can black olives,
  drained and diced
1 tomato, diced
4 teaspoons sour cream

In a large skillet brown ground beef, drain grease. Add taco seasoning; prepare according to package directions. Stir in Ranch style beans, set aside to cool. Layer lettuce in Taco Shell Bowls or on plate. Spoon beef mixture on lettuce. Top with salsa, cheese, green onions, olives, tomato, and sour cream.

Makes 4 servings   Mild

Immigrants smuggled tomato seeds into the United States.

Taco Shell Bowl

Preheat oven to 350 degrees

2 (8 inch) flour tortilla
Vegetable spray

In a medium bowl, soak flour tortillas in warm water for 1 minute. Place 2 oven safe cereal bowls on a baking sheet upside down, spray bottom and sides with vegetable spray. Place wet tortillas on upside down sprayed bowls. Take 2 more cereal bowls; spray the inside with vegetable spray and place on top of wet tortilla. Bake for 30 minutes. As the shell cools it will become crisp. Remove from oven, take top bowl off and cool tortilla shell while still on bottom bowl. When cool remove and fill with your favorite salad recipe.

Makes 2 servings

Fajita Salad

1 1/2 pounds chicken breast,
  cut into 1/2 inch strips
2 tablespoons vegetable oil, divided
2 cloves garlic, minced
2 tablespoons minced cilantro
1 tablespoon lime juice
1/2 teaspoon salt
1/4 teaspoon black pepper
2 Jalapeno peppers, seeded and chopped
2 green onions, chopped with tops
1/2 teaspoon red pepper flakes
1 head iceberg lettuce, shredded
2 tomatoes, chopped
2 avocados, chopped
3/4 cup salsa
1/2 cup sour cream

The top countries producing tomatoes are the United States, China, Turkey, Italy, and India.

In a medium glass bowl combine chicken strips, 1 tablespoon vegetable oil, garlic, cilantro, lime juice, salt, and black pepper, mix well. Refrigerate for 3 hours. In a large skillet over medium high heat sauté Jalapeno peppers, onion, and red pepper flakes in remaining vegetable oil for 3 minutes. Remove pepper mixture form skillet, set aside. Place chicken in skillet and brown. Return Jalapeno mixture to skillet with chicken; sauté until mixture is warm. Place lettuce on plates, top with chicken mixture, top with tomatoes, avocados, salsa, and sour cream.

Makes 6 servings   Mild

Rio Rice Salad

3 cups cooked rice
9 hard boiled eggs, chopped
1 cup chopped celery
1/2 cup chopped with tops green onions
1 (4 ounce) can diced green chiles
1 cup shredded cheddar cheese
1 cup sour cream
1 tablespoon lemon juice
1/4 cup salsa
2 teaspoons salt
1 teaspoon pepper
1 tomato, chopped

In a large bowl, combine rice, egg, celery, onion, chiles, and cheese. In a small bowl, combine sour cream, lemon juice, salsa, salt and pepper. Mix well. Pour dressing over rice mixture toss to coat. Top with tomato.

Makes 6 servings   Mild

Florida, California, and Georgia are the states that produce the most tomatoes.

Avocado and Rice Salad

3 cups cooked rice
2 cups cooked and diced chicken
1 (4 ounce) can diced green chiles
1/2 cup diced ham
1/4 cup sliced black olives
2 tablespoons mayonnaise
1 tablespoon diced onion
4 avocados, halved
1 teaspoon lemon juice

In a medium bowl combine all ingredients except avocados and lemon juice, mix well. Cut avocados in half. Remove peel and seed. Place avocado on individual plates, lightly brush with lemon juice. Spoon rice mixture into avocados and serve.

Makes 8 servings   Mild

Extra Mild Version: *Exchange the chiles for 1/2 cup diced celery.*

Over 35 million backyard gardens grow tomatoes in the United States.

Spicy Rice Salad

1 cup cooked rice
6 tablespoons olive oil
3 tablespoons red wine vinegar
1 (4 ounce) can diced green chiles
1/2 cup chopped cucumber
1/4 cup chopped red bell pepper
1/4 cup diced with tops, green onion
2 tablespoons minced cilantro
1 teaspoon salt
1/4 teaspoon chili powder

In a medium size bowl, combine all ingredients, mix well. Serve chilled.

Makes 4 Servings   Medium

Mild Version: *Replace green chiles with 1/2 cup green bell pepper.*

Texas Tomato Salad

4 tomatoes
4 fresh Big John green chile peppers
1 cup peas
1/2 teaspoon minced cilantro
1/2 teaspoon lemon juice

Peel, seed, and cut tomatoes and peppers into strips. In a medium bowl combine all ingredients, toss gently. Cover and chill for 30 minutes.

Makes 4 Servings   Wild & Hot

Mild Version: Exchange Big John Green chile peppers for 1 can of mild green chiles.

'I will not move my army without onions!'
Ulysses S. Grant

Marinated Tomato Salad

4 large tomatoes, chopped
1 red onion, chopped
1 cucumber, chopped
1 green bell pepper, chopped
1/3 cup minced parsley or cilantro

Marinade
1/3 cup apple cider vinegar
2 cloves garlic, minced
1 tablespoon olive oil
1 teaspoon sugar
1/2 teaspoon salt
1/4 teaspoon black pepper

In a medium bowl combine tomatoes, onion, cucumber, bell pepper, and parsley or cilantro. In a small bowl blend cider, garlic, olive oil, sugar, salt, and black pepper, mix well. Pour marinade over vegetables, toss to cover. Chill 1 hour before serving.

Makes 6 servings   Mild

Salsa Salad

9 tomatoes, chopped
7 avocados, peeled and diced
3 onions, chopped
2/3 cup olive oil
1/3 cup lemon juice
1/2 cup chopped cilantro
5 Jalapeno chiles, seeded and chopped
3 cloves garlic, minced

In a large bowl combine all ingredients.
Cover and refrigerate.

Makes 8 servings   Wild & Hot

*Mild Version: Eliminate the Jalapeno peppers.
Use 1/4 cup canned mild diced peppers.*

'Onion skins very thin, Mild winter coming in. Onion skins very tough, Coming winter very rough.' Old English rhyme.

Crabby Avocado Salad

1 (6 ounce) can crab meat
1/2 cup chopped celery
4 tablespoons lemon juice, divided
2 tablespoons mayonnaise
1 tablespoon salsa
3 avocados, peeled, seeded, halved

In a small bowl combine, crab meat, celery,
2 tablespoons lemon juice, mayonnaise, and
salsa, mix well. Sprinkle remaining lemon juice
over avocado halves. Spoon crab mixture onto
avocados and serve.

Makes 6 servings   Mild

Camaron Salad

1 head lettuce, shredded
12 medium sized shrimp, cooked
1 avocado, chopped
1 cup peas
10 green onions, chopped with tops
4 tablespoons Parmesan cheese
$1/2$ cup vinegar
4 tablespoons vegetable oil
4 (6 inch) corn tortillas
1 cup refried beans
1 cup shredded cheddar cheese

In a large bowl combine lettuce, shrimp, avocado, peas, onion, Parmesan cheese, vinegar, and oil, mix well. Heat tortilla in microwave for 20 seconds or until warm. Place tortillas on individual plates. Spread refried beans on each tortilla, sprinkle with cheddar cheese. Top with lettuce mixture and serve.

Makes 4 servings   Mild

 "Life is like an onion. You peel it off one layer at a time; and sometimes you weep." Carl Sandburg, American poet

Santa Fe Turkey Salad

1/4 pound turkey breast tenderloins,
    skinless and boneless
1 (1.25 ounce) package taco seasoning
1/4 cup salsa, chilled
2 tablespoons sour cream
1 tablespoon chopped cilantro
1 large head romaine lettuce

Sprinkle turkey breast with taco seasoning; fry in a large skillet until turkey is no longer pink in the center. In a small bowl mix salsa, sour cream, and cilantro together. Tear the lettuce into bit size pieces and place on a plate. Slice turkey breast into strips and lay on top of salad. Drizzle the salsa mixture over each salad and serve

Makes 4 servings   Mild

"Onions can make even heirs and widows weep."
Benjamin Franklin

Gazpacho Salad

3 3/4 cups sliced mushrooms
1 cup diced tomato
1 cup diced cucumber
3/4 cup diced green pepper
3/4 cup diced red onion
1 recipe Chile Dressing

In a medium bowl combine all ingredients. Toss to coat vegetables. Serve chilled.

Makes 6 servings   Mild

Chile Dressing

1/2 cup olive oil
3 tablespoons red wine vinegar
3/4 teaspoon chili powder
3/4 teaspoon salt
1/4 teaspoon black pepper
1 clove garlic, minced

In a small bowl, combine all ingredients.
Serve chilled.

Makes 3/4 Cup   Medium

Ancho Salad

2 tablespoons olive oil
1 Ancho pepper, reserve sauce
1/4 teaspoon fennel seed
1/4 teaspoon ground cumin
1/4 teaspoon salt
4 tomatoes, sliced
1 tablespoon lime juice
2 tablespoons minced cilantro

In a small saucepan over medium heat,
warm olive oil. Add Ancho pepper, fennel,
cumin, and salt, simmer for 1 minute. Set
aside to cool, discard pepper. Arrange
tomatoes on platter, sprinkle with lime
juice. Top with Ancho sauce.

Makes 4 servings   Medium

 Eating chile peppers is addicting. The brain releases endorphins, the bodies natural pain killers, when capsaicin comes in contact with nerves in your mouth.

Cilantro Salad

3/4 cup salsa
1/4 cup chopped cilantro
1/4 cup lime juice
2 tablespoons olive oil
2 cups chopped tomatoes
1 cup chopped zucchini
1 avocado, peeled, seeded, chopped
1 (15 ounce) can kidney beans,
   rinsed and drained
1 (4 ounce) can diced green chiles

In a large bowl, combine salsa, cilantro, lime juice, and olive oil. Stir in tomatoes, zucchini, avocado, kidney beans, and green chiles, mix well. Cover and refrigerate for 2 hours.

Makes 6 servings   Mild

To ripen tomatoes, place them in a brown paper bag. Close the end and leave at room temperature.

Pepper Salad

3 green bell peppers, seeded and chopped
3 red bell peppers, seeded and chopped
1/2 cup vegetable oil
1/4 cup cider vinegar
1/4 cup sugar
2 cloves garlic, minced
1/2 teaspoon salt
1/4 teaspoon black pepper

In a large skillet over medium high heat, sauté peppers in oil until slightly browned. Reduce heat, add vinegar, sugar, garlic, salt, and pepper; cook until bell pepper is soft. Refrigerate for 2 hours.

Makes 8 servings   Mild

Zesty Zucchini Salad

1/2 cup olive oil
5 tablespoons white vinegar
1 clove garlic, minced
1/4 teaspoon oregano
2 zucchinis, sliced to bite size
1 cup garbanzo beans, drained
1/2 cup sliced black olives
3 green onions, chopped with tops
1 avocado, chopped
1/2 cup shredded mozzarella cheese
1 chipotle in adobo sauce, minced
1 head lettuce, shredded

In a medium bowl, combine olive oil, vinegar, garlic, and oregano, mix well. Add zucchini, garbanzo beans, black olives, and green onions, toss to coat. Refrigerate for 30 minutes. Before serving add avocado, cheese, and chipotle, toss to coat. Serve on a bed of lettuce.

Makes 6 Servings   Mild

The largest producers of olive oil are Spain, Italy, Greece, Portugal, and Tunisia.

Amarillo Avocado Salad

1 (10 ounce) can whole cranberry sauce
1/2 cup diced celery
3 avocados, peeled, seeded, and halved
1/2 cup chopped pecans

In a small bowl combine cranberries and celery. Spoon cranberry mixture into hollow in avocado. Top with pecans.

Makes 6 servings   Mild

South of the Border Salad

1 (7 ounce) can green chile salsa
1 1/2 cups mayonnaise
1/3 cup catsup
1/2 teaspoon chili powder
1 1/2 heads romaine lettuce, shredded
2 (2.25 ounce) cans sliced black olives
1 (4 ounce) can diced green chiles
3 tomatoes, diced
1/2 cup shredded cheddar cheese
2 avocados, diced
3 cups crushed tortilla chips

In a small bowl combine, green chile salsa, mayonnaise, catsup, and chili powder, mix well. In individual bowls layer lettuce evenly, black olives, green chiles, tomatoes. Spread mayonnaise dressing on top. Sprinkle cheese, avocado, and tortilla chips on mayonnaise dressing and serve.

Make 6 Servings   Mild

Cilantro will stay fresh up to a week by wrapping it in paper towels, place into a sealed plastic bag and store in the refrigerator.

El Fuerte Egg Salad

4 hard cooked eggs, chopped
1 cup shredded cheddar cheese
1/4 cup salad dressing
3 tablespoons diced green chiles
2 tablespoons chopped onion
2 tablespoons chopped green pepper
2 cups tortilla chips

In a medium bowl, combine egg, cheese, dressing, chiles, onion, and green pepper, mix well. Serve with tortilla chips.

Makes 2 servings   Mild

Colima Chopped Salad

1/2 cup salsa
1/2 cup plain yogurt
1 tablespoon + 1 teaspoon mayonnaise
2 teaspoons lime juice
2 teaspoons red wine vinegar
2 1/2 cups shredded green cabbage
8 ounces cooked black beans, drained
1/2 cup diced red onion
1/2 cup shredded carrot
1/4 cup chopped parsley

In a small bowl, combine salsa, yogurt, mayonnaise, lime juice, and vinegar to make dressing, stir well. In a medium bowl, combine cabbage, beans, onion, carrot, and parsley. Pour dressing over cabbage mixture, toss well. Refrigerate 2 hours

Makes 6 servings   Mild

Tear lettuce instead of using a knife to keep the lettuce from browning on the edges.

Mexican Coleslaw

3/4 pound bunch spinach, cut into 1/2 inch wide strips
2 medium red peppers, cut into 1/2 inch wide strips
1 (16 ounce) package shredded cabbage coleslaw mix
2 (16 ounce) cans red kidney beans, drained, rinsed
1 (8 ounce) package shredded mozzarella cheese
1/2 cup vinaigrette salad dressing

In a large bowl combine all ingredients. Mix well.

Makes 8 servings   Mild

Vista Salad

2 (11 ounce) cans Mexican style corn,
  drained
1 (15 ounce) can black beans,
  rinsed and drained
1 (4 ounce) can sliced mushrooms,
  drained
1 tomato, seeded and chopped
1/2 cup chopped onion
1/4 cup minced cilantro
3 cloves garlic, minced
1 Jalapeno pepper, seeded and chopped
1/4 cup olive oil
2 tablespoons red wine vinegar
1 tablespoon lime juice
1 teaspoon chili powder
1 teaspoon ground cumin
1/2 teaspoon salt

In a large mixing bowl combine, corn, beans, mushrooms, tomato, onion, cilantro, garlic, and Jalapeno pepper; mix well. In a small bowl combine, olive oil, vinegar, lime juice, chili powder, cumin, and salt. Pour olive oil mixture over salad mixture; toss to coat. Chill 30 minutes before serving.

Makes 10 servings   Wild & Hot

Mild Version: Eliminate Jalapeno pepper. Reduce chile and cumin powder to 1/4 teaspoon each.

When buying garlic choose heads that are firm and heavy. Garlic that has a purple hue will be more pungent.

Fruit Salad

6 cups salad greens, torn
3 navel oranges, peeled and sectioned
2 grapefruits, peeled and sectioned
1 avocado, peeled and sliced
$1/4$ cup slivered and toasted almonds

Dressing
$1/2$ cup vegetable oil
$1/3$ cup sugar
3 tablespoons vinegar
2 teaspoons poppy seeds
1 teaspoon finely chopped onion
$1/2$ teaspoon salt
$1/2$ teaspoon ground mustard

In a large bowl, toss salad greens, oranges, grapefruit, avocado, and almonds. In a jar or container with a well fitting lid, add all dressing ingredients; shake well. Pour dressing over salad and toss to coat.

Makes 6 servings   Mild

 To store a cut avocado, leave seed in the center and coat edges with mayonnaise or butter or sprinkle with lemon juice.

Fiesta Fruit Salad

3 oranges, peeled and sectioned
1 grapefruit, peeled and sectioned
1 (16 ounce) can red kidney beans,
   rinsed and drained
1 cup celery, chopped
3 tablespoons chopped pimiento
2 tablespoons chopped parsley
1/4 cup salad oil
3 tablespoons orange juice
2 tablespoons minced onion
1 teaspoon salt
1/2 teaspoon oregano
1/2 teaspoon thyme

Salad dressing is good for three months if stored in the refrigerator.

Cut orange and grapefruit slices into bite size pieces. In a medium bowl, combine orange, grapefruit, beans, celery, pimento, and parsley. In a small bowl combine oil, orange juice, onion, salt, oregano, and thyme, mix well. Pour dressing over salad, toss to coat. Refrigerate for 1 hour before serving.

Makes 6 servings   Mild

Mexicano Potato Salad

1/3 cup white wine vinegar
3 tablespoons olive oil
2 cloves garlic, minced
1/2 teaspoon salt
1/4 teaspoon pepper
1 1/2 pounds potatoes, cooked and diced
1 apple, cored and finely chopped
1 (4 ounce) can diced green chiles
1 (2 ounce) can black olives,
   drained and diced
1/4 cup diced red onion
8 strips bacon, cooked

In a small bowl, combine vinegar, olive oil, garlic, salt, and pepper. In a large bowl, combine potatoes, apple, green chiles, black olives, red onion. Crumble 7 pieces of bacon into the potato mixture. Add vinegar mixture to the potato mixture, mix well. Crumble remaining strip of bacon on top of salad. Chill 1 hour before serving.

Makes 6 servings   Mild

Potatoes boiled or baked in their skins will retain most of their vitamins and minerals. Halving or peeling causes nutrient loss.

Mexican Potato Salad

6 cups peeled, cooked,
  and cubed potatoes
1 1/2 cups shredded cheddar cheese
2/3 cup chopped red pepper
2/3 cup black beans, drained and rinsed
1/2 cup chopped celery
1/3 cup chopped green onions
1 tablespoon minced cilantro
3/4 cup ranch salad dressing
1/2 cup salsa
1/2 teaspoon salt

In a large bowl, combine potatoes, cheese, red pepper, black beans, celery, onions, and cilantro. In a small bowl, combine salad dressing, salsa, and salt. Pour dressing mixture over potatoes and toss to coat. Cover and refrigerate for at least 1 hour.

Makes 14 servings   Mild

Place cilantro in a glass measuring cup and cut into pieces by using kitchen shears.

Gringo Pasta Salad

1 (12 ounce) package colored spiral pasta
1/2 cup mayonnaise
1/2 cup sour cream
1 (1.25 ounce) package taco seasoning

Boil pasta until tender. Drain and rinse with cold water. In a large bowl add cooled pasta, mayonnaise, and sour cream, mix well. Sprinkle dry taco seasoning over pasta mixture, mix well. Refrigerate 2 hours

Makes 6 servings   Mild

Jalapeno Pasta Salad

1¼ pounds spiral pasta, cooked
1½ tablespoons plus ⅓ cup olive oil
7 cups chicken, cooked and shredded
4 tomatoes, chopped
3 cups canned corn, drained
3 carrots, sliced thinly
¼ cup diced red onion
3 Jalapeno peppers, seeded and
   chopped
½ cup minced cilantro
2½ tablespoons lime juice
2½ tablespoons Dijon style mustard
1¼ teaspoons ground cumin
1¼ teaspoons chili powder

In a large bowl, add 1½ tablespoons olive oil to cooked and drained pasta, toss to coat. Mix in chicken, tomatoes, corn, carrots, onion, Jalapeno peppers, and cilantro. In a small bowl combine ⅓ cup olive oil, lime juice, mustard, cumin and chili powder, mix well. Pour mustard mixture over pasta, mix well. Cover and chill for 1 hour.

Makes 8 servings   Wild & Hot

Mild Version: Eliminate Jalapeno peppers. Reduce chili powder to ¼ teaspoon.

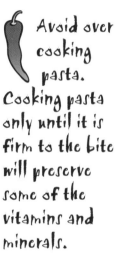

Avoid over cooking pasta. Cooking pasta only until it is firm to the bite will preserve some of the vitamins and minerals.

Fiery Pasta Salad

1 (12 ounce) package colored spiral pasta
1/2 cup chile sauce
3/4 cup mayonnaise
2 tablespoons vinegar
2 teaspoons chili powder
2 teaspoons onion salt
5 drops hot pepper sauce
1 (14 ounce) can kidney beans,
   drained and rinsed
1/4 cup chopped onion
1/2 cup sliced black olives

Boil pasta until tender. Drain and rinse with cold water. In a large bowl combine chile sauce, mayonnaise, vinegar, chili powder, onion salt, and hot pepper sauce. Add pasta, kidney beans, onion, and black olives. Cover, chill 2 hours before serving.

Makes 10 servings   Wild & Hot

Mild Version: *Eliminate the hot pepper sauce and chili powder. Use 1/2 cup tomato sauce instead of the chile sauce.*

When substituting fresh herbs for dry, use three times more fresh as dried to get the same flavor.

Out of Control

Meat, Chicken & Fish

Sizzling Steak Burritos

1 tablespoon oil
12 ounce flank steak
1 fresh Jalapeno pepper,
   seeded and chopped
4 (10 inch) flour tortillas
2 cups shredded lettuce
1 1/2 cups grated Monterey Jack cheese
1 avocado, sliced thinly
3/4 cup salsa
3/4 cup chopped tomato
3/4 cup chopped black olives
1/2 cup chopped onion
3/4 cup sour cream

In a large skillet, add oil, steak, and the Jalapeno pepper. Brown over medium heat until desired doneness. Transfer cooked steak to a cutting board and cut into thin strips. Heat tortillas in the microwave for 20 seconds or in a skillet over medium heat, until it is heated throughout. Place tortilla on a plate, fill with the steak and remaining ingredients. Repeat the process until all tortillas are used.

Makes 4 servings   Wild & Hot

Mild Version: Delete the Jalapeno pepper from the recipe. Salt and pepper the steak instead. Use mild salsa.

Many of today's most popular Mexican dishes were created during the colonial times by Nuns, such as chiles rellenos and guacamole.

San Antonio Steak

2 tablespoons flour
1/2 teaspoon salt
1/4 teaspoon pepper
1 1/2 pounds round steak, cut in cubes
2 (4 ounce) cans diced green chile
1 (15 ounce) can tomato sauce

Combine flour, salt, and pepper. Dredge steak in flour mixture, place in crock pot. Top with green chiles and tomato sauce. Cover and cook on low 8 to 10 hours or on high 4 to 5 hours

Makes 6 servings   Mild

A former Austrian archduke Ferdinand Maximilian was kept in power between 1864 and 1897 by French troops. French cooking left its mark on many Mexican dishes and baked items.

Burrol Mountain Beef Burritos

1/2 pound lean ground beef
1 cup chopped onion
1 (10 ounce) can tomatoes with green
   chile peppers
1 (15 ounce) can black beans, drained
   and rinsed
2 teaspoons chili powder
4 (10 inch) flour tortillas

In a large skillet, brown beef and onion over medium high heat. Drain grease. Stir in tomatoes, black beans, and chili powder. Bring to a boil then reduce heat and simmer 5 minutes. Heat tortillas in microwave for 30 seconds to soften. Spoon 1/4 cup meat mixture down the center of each tortilla, roll to close.

Makes 4 servings   Medium

Chili Sauce Steaks

1/2 cup red wine vinegar
2 tablespoons soy sauce
1 clove garlic, minced
5 (4 ounce) beef tenderloin steaks
1/4 cup chili sauce
1/4 cup seedless red raspberry jam
1 tablespoon honey mustard
1 tablespoon water

In a large plastic bag, combine vinegar, soy sauce, and garlic. Place steak in bag and refrigerate at least 1 hour. After 30 minutes turn bag over. Remove steak and discard marinade. Grill or broil steaks to desired doneness. In a small saucepan over medium heat, combine chili sauce, jam, mustard, and water. Simmer 5 minutes. Pour sauce over steaks and serve.

Makes 5 servings   Mild

Enchiladas are a Tex-Mex classic. It is a blend of Native American, Texas cowboy, and Mexican cooking.

Salsa Steak

1/2 cup red wine vinegar
2 tablespoons olive oil
2 teaspoons chili powder
2 teaspoons crushed red pepper
1 clove garlic, minced
1 teaspoon salt
1/2 teaspoon pepper
4 boneless chuck eye steaks
1 cup salsa

Between 1985 and 1990, Mexican style sauces sales grew seventy five percent.

In a large plastic bag, combine vinegar, olive oil, chili powder, red pepper, garlic, salt, and pepper. Place steak in bag, shake to coat. Marinade at least 8 hours or over night. Turn bag over during marinating time. Remove steak, reserve marinade. Grill steak to desired doneness, basting with marinate while grilling. Top with salsa and serve.

Makes 4 servings   Medium

Riodoso Round Steak

1 1/2 pounds round steak,
  cut in 1 inch strips
1/2 cup chopped onions
1 (15 ounce) Mexican style stewed
  tomatoes
2 green peppers, seeded and cut in strips

In a large skillet over medium heat, brown meat. Stir in onion, tomatoes, and green peppers. Cover and simmer for 1 hour.

Makes 4 servings   Mild

Tourist Pot Roast

2 1/2 pounds boneless beef chuck roast
1 (14 1/2 ounces) can tomatoes,
   diced with juice
1 onion, chopped
1/2 cup white vinegar
3 tablespoons tomato paste
2 teaspoons Dijon mustard
1/2 teaspoon lemon juice
4 1/2 teaspoons poppy seeds
2 1/4 teaspoons sugar
2 cloves garlic, minced
1/2 teaspoon rosemary, crushed
1/2 teaspoon ground ginger
1/2 teaspoon red pepper flakes
1/2 teaspoon salt
1/4 teaspoon turmeric
1/4 teaspoon cumin
1/8 teaspoon ground cloves
1 bay leaf
4 cups cooked rice

In a crock pot, place roast. In a large bowl, combine remaining ingredients except rice, mix well. Pour over pot roast. Cover and cook on low for 8 to 9 hours. Serve over rice.

Makes 8 servings   Mild

 In 1941 red taco sauce, green taco sauce, and enchilada sauce were introduced in the United States.

Roswell Roast

Preheat oven to 325 degrees

3 pounds boneless round roast
1/4 cup flour
1 (16 ounce) jar thick and chunky salsa
1 clove garlic, minced
7 carrots, cut in 2 inch pieces
4 red potatoes, quartered
1 green bell pepper, cut in strips
1 onion, cut in thin wedges

Coat roast with flour. Place roast in 13 x 9 inch baking dish. Pour salsa over roast. Arrange vegetables around roast. Cover and bake 2 hours.

Makes 8 servings   Mild

As a general rule, the smaller the pepper is the hotter the flavor is.

Santa Fe Beef and Vegetables

Preheat oven to 450 degrees

1/2 pound boneless beef sirloin steak, cubed
1 1/2 teaspoons Santa Fe seasoning
1 (8 3/4 ounce) can corn, drained
1 zucchini, sliced 1/4 inch thick
1 red bell pepper, cut in strips
1/3 cup prepared beef gravy
1/2 teaspoon salt

In an 8 x 8 inch baking dish, place beef and sprinkle 1/2 teaspoon Santa Fe seasoning. Arrange vegetables over meat. Mix remaining Santa Fe seasoning and salt into gravy. Pour gravy over vegetables. Cover and bake 25 minutes.

Makes 4 servings   Mild

Mexican Meatloaf

Preheat oven to 450 degrees

1 pound extra lean ground beef
1/4 onion, chopped
1/4 cup crushed tortilla chips
2 teaspoons Worcestershire sauce
2 teaspoons chili powder
1/2 teaspoon garlic salt
3/4 cup salsa, divided
1 (15 1/4 ounce) whole kernel corn,
  drained

Combine the first six ingredients and 1/4 cup of salsa. Place into a large loaf pan or two small loaf pans. Top meat mixture with corn and remaining salsa. Bake for 45 minutes.

Makes 4 servings   Medium

Mild Version: Use 1/4 teaspoon of chili powder and mild salsa.

 Anaheim: Referred to as green chile. It ranges in size from 6 to 7 inches and is pointed. Green in color. Mild to medium flavor.

San Juan Stuffed Meatloaf

Preheat oven to 375 degrees

2 pounds lean ground beef
1 (8 ounce) can tomato sauce
1 (1½ ounce) taco seasoning
⅓ cup chopped onion
⅓ cup chopped green pepper
2 slices white bread, crumbled
1 large egg, beaten
3 cups shredded cheddar cheese
½ cup sour cream

Ancho: Dried Poblano chile. Dark red to purple in color. Sweet flavor.

In a large bowl, combine beef, tomato sauce, taco seasoning, onion, pepper, bread, and egg. In a small bowl, combine 2 cups cheese and sour cream, mix well. Place half of meat mixture in a 9 x 5 inch loaf pan. Make a deep well in the center of the meat mixture. Spoon cheese mixture evenly in well. Place remaining meat mixture in loaf pan. Cover cheese mixture completely, seal edges. Bake for 1 hour 30 minutes. Sprinkle 1 cup cheddar cheese on top of loaf. Bake an additional 5 minutes or until cheese is completely melted.

Makes 8 servings   Mild

Tijuana Taco Burgers

1½ pounds ground beef
1 (1.25 ounce) package taco seasoning
¼ cup catsup
¼ cup milk

In a large bowl, combine all ingredients. Shape into 6 patties. Grill or fry.

Makes 6 servings   Mild

Maraca Meatloaf

Preheat oven to 350 degrees

2 pounds ground beef
15 saltine crackers, crushed
1 onion, chopped
2 cups chile sauce, divided

In a large bowl, combine beef, crackers, onion, and 1 cup chile sauce, mix well. In a 9 x 13 inch baking pan, shape meat into a loaf. Pour remaining chile sauce over loaf. Bake for 1¹/₂ hours.

Makes 6 servings   Mild.

Salsa Patties

1 pound ground beef
¹/₂ cup breadcrumbs
1 tablespoon salsa
1 tablespoon minced green onion
¹/₂ teaspoon salt
¹/₄ teaspoon pepper

In a large bowl, combine all ingredients, mix well. Shape into 4 patties. Grill or fry.

Makes 4 servings   Mild

Cayenne: Small and thin in size. Bright red in color. Very hot flavor.

Queso Burgers

8 hamburger patties, cooked as desired
1 cup shredded cheddar cheese
1/4 cup salsa
8 hamburger buns

Place cooked hamburgers on a baking sheet. In a small bowl, combine cheese and salsa. Evenly divide cheese mixture on top of hamburger patties. Broil until cheese is melted. Place patties on buns and serve.

Makes 8 servings   Mild

Chipotle: Dried and smoked Jalapeno pepper. Dark brown in color. Have a smoky, chocolate flavor.

Chili Burgers

1½ pounds ground beef
1 (3 ounce) package chili seasoning mix
1 cup shredded cheddar cheese
6 hamburger buns

In a large bowl, combine ground beef, chili seasoning, and cheese. Shape into 6 patties. Grill or fry to desired doneness.

Makes 6 servings   Mild

Taco Burgers

1½ pounds ground beef
1 (1.5 ounce) package taco seasoning
1/4 cup salsa
1/4 cup milk
6 hamburger buns
6 slices processed cheese

In a large bowl, combine beef, taco seasoning, salsa, and milk. Make into 6 patties. Grill or fry to desired doneness. Place cheese on each patties, place on buns and serve.

Makes 6 servings   Mild

Pancho Patties

1 pound ground beef
1/2 cup flavored bread crumbs
1 tablespoon chopped green onions
1 tablespoon salsa
1/2 cup shredded cheddar cheese

In a large bowl, combine beef, bread crumbs, onions, and salsa. Shape into 4 patties. Grill or fry to desired doneness. Top with cheese and serve.

Makes 4 servings   Mild

Sloppy Jose Burgers

1 pound lean ground beef
1 fresh Jalapeno pepper, seeded and chopped
1 onion, minced
1 cup salsa
1 (4 ounce) can tomato paste
1 teaspoon chili powder
1/2 teaspoon cumin
1/2 teaspoon black pepper
1/2 teaspoon seasoned salt
1/2 clove garlic, minced
6 hamburger buns

In a large skillet brown beef over medium high heat. Drain grease. Reduce heat and add all remaining ingredients. Cover and simmer for 10 minutes. Spoon mixture onto hamburger buns and serve.

Makes 6 servings   Wild & Hot

Mild Version: Eliminate the Jalapeno pepper and the cumin. Reduce the chili powder to 1/4 teaspoon. Use Mild salsa.

Habanera: Small in size. Range from green to orange in color. Hottest pepper known.

Peppy Pitas

Preheat oven to 350 degrees

2 pounds ground beef
1 (1 ounce) package taco seasoning
1/3 cup water
**1 (10 ounce) can diced tomatoes and green
    chiles, undrained**
1 (16 ounce) refried beans
7 (6 inch) pitas, halved
3 cups shredded cheddar cheese
1/4 cup sliced Jalapeno peppers

In a large skillet over medium high heat, brown beef, drain. Reduce heat and add taco seasoning and water simmer 5 minutes. Add tomatoes, green chiles and refried beans, mix well. Simmer uncovered for 20 minutes. Spoon approximately 1/3 cup into each halved pita. Top with cheese and Jalapeno peppers. Place pitas in 13 x 9 x 2 inch baking dish. Bake uncovered for 15 minutes or until cheese is melted.

Makes 14 pitas   Medium

Mild Version: Exchange a 4 ounce can of green chiles for Jalapeno peppers.

Jalapeno: Small and plump in size. Dark green in color. Hot flavor.

Ring Around the Taco

Preheat oven to 375 degrees

1 pound lean ground beef
1 (1.25 ounce) package taco seasoning
1 cup shredded cheddar cheese
2 (8 ounce) packages crescent rolls
3 cups shredded lettuce
1 tomato, chopped
1/4 cup chopped onion
1/4 cup sour cream

In a large skillet over medium high heat, brown ground beef. Drain grease. Add taco seasoning to beef, prepare according to package. Mix cheese into beef, set aside. On a large cookie sheet, place crescent rolls in a circle with points on the inside and wide edge on the outside. Scoop beef mixture onto each crescent roll. Fold point over beef, meat mixture will not be completely covered. Bake for 20 minutes or until golden brown. Place in a ring on a serving dish. Layer lettuce, tomato, onion, and sour cream in the center of ring. Cut into wedges and serve.

Makes 12 servings   Mild

 Pablano: Medium in size. Dark green in color. Most commonly used for stuffing. Medium to hot flavor.

Shredded Beef Tacos

1½ pounds beef chuck roast
1 onion, chopped
1 (1.25 ounce) package taco seasoning
1 cup water
1 (16 ounce) jar salsa
1 (7 ounce) can green chiles, diced
12 hard taco shells

Place beef and onion in a crock pot. In a small bowl, combine taco seasoning and water, pour over beef. Cook on low 6 to 8 hours. Remove beef, shred and place in a large bowl. Stir in salsa and chiles. Microwave taco shells for 40 seconds or until warm. Serve with lettuce, cheese, tomato, onion, and avocado.

Makes 6 servings   Mild

Climate and soil conditions affect the heat in chiles.

Taquitos

2 pounds beef brisket
2 cups water
3 beef bouillon cubes
4 cloves garlic, minced
1 tablespoon red pepper flakes
18 corn tortillas

Place brisket in crock pot. Add water, bouillon cubes, garlic, red pepper flakes. Cook for 4 hours on high. Drain water from beef then shred beef. Wrap tortillas in wet paper towel, microwave for 40 seconds until soft. Place beef down center of each tortilla. Roll up tightly, to form a long cylinder. Secure tortilla edge with a toothpick. Deep fry in 2 inches of vegetable oil. Drain on paper towel.

Make 9 servings   Mild

Taos Taco Bake

Preheat oven to 375 degrees

1 pound lean ground beef
1 (1.25 ounce) package taco seasoning
1 cup shredded cheddar cheese
1 cup sour cream
3/4 cup mayonnaise
2 tablespoons chopped onion
2 cups Bisquick® baking mix
1/2 cup water
2 tomatoes, thinly sliced
1 cup chopped green pepper

In a large skillet, brown ground beef, drain grease; add taco seasoning and 3/4 cup water or the amount recommended on the package. In a small bowl, mix cheese, sour cream, mayonnaise, and onion, set aside. Put Bisquick® mix in a medium bowl and add water until soft dough forms. Pat dough into a greased 9 x 13 inch pan, pressing dough 1/2 inch up the sides. Layer beef, tomatoes and green pepper over dough. Spoon sour cream mixture over top. Bake until edges of dough are light brown, approximately 35 minutes.

Makes 8 servings   Mild

Serranos: Dark green color to dark red when ripe. Medium to hot flavor.

Beefy Quesadillas

Preheat oven to 475 degrees

2¹/₂ cups cooked and shredded beef

²/₃ cup salsa

¹/₃ cup, chopped with tops, green onions

1 teaspoon ground cumin

¹/₂ teaspoon ground red pepper

¹/₂ teaspoon salt

6 (8 inch) flour tortillas

¹/₄ cup butter or margarine, melted

1 (8 ounce) package Monterey Jack
    cheese, shredded

¹/₂ cup sour cream

Slice quesadillas with a pizza cutter.

In a skillet over medium heat, combine beef, salsa, onions, cumin, red pepper, and salt. Cook uncovered for 10 minutes. Brush one side of tortilla with butter. Divide beef evenly onto 3 tortillas. Sprinkle with cheese. Top with buttered tortilla. Bake for 10 minutes. Serve with sour cream.

Makes 6 servings   Mild

Tortilla Stack

Preheat oven to 350 degrees

1 pound lean ground beef
1 cup chopped red bell pepper
1 cup chopped onion
1 cup salsa
1 teaspoon chili powder
6 (6 inch) corn tortillas
**4 ounces Monterey Jack cheese,
  shredded**
1 cup sour cream
1 cup canned corn, drained

In a large skillet over medium heat, brown beef, onion, and 2/3 cup red pepper. Drain grease. Stir in salsa and chili powder, simmer 5 minutes. Spray a 9 inch pie pan with cooking spray. Layer 2 tortillas on bottom of plate, top with 1/3 cup meat mixture, 1/3 cup sour cream, and 1/3 cup cheese. Repeat process to make 3 layers. Use foil to cover sides. Top stack with remaining red pepper and corn. Bake for 25 minutes.

Makes 8 servings   Medium

 The riper the chile is, the hotter the flavor will be.

Festive Fajitas

1 (1 ounce) packet ranch dressing mix
2 tablespoons olive oil
1 tablespoon water
1½ pounds flank steak, cut into thin strips
1½ cups sliced onion
1½ cups sliced green pepper
4 (10 inch) flour tortillas
1 avocado, peeled, pitted, thinly sliced
½ cup sour cream
½ cup chopped tomato

In a small bowl combine, dressing, oil, and water, mix well. In a large skillet over medium high heat, sauté steak in dressing mixture. Add onion and pepper strips, cook until onion is tender. In a microwave, heat tortillas for 30 seconds. Place steak mixture on tortillas, serve with avocado, sour cream and tomato.

Makes 4 servings   Mild

Marinated Steak Fajitas

3 tablespoons olive oil
1 tablespoon red wine vinegar
1½ teaspoons dried oregano
1 teaspoon chili powder
1 (2 pound) flank steak, thinly sliced
1 large green pepper, thinly sliced
1 large onion, thinly sliced
8 large flour tortillas

In a large heavy-duty resealable plastic bag, combine oil, vinegar, oregano, and chili powder. Place steak in bag, press out air and seal. Refrigerate overnight. Discard marinade from the steak. In a large skillet over medium high heat, brown steak, peppers and onions. Microwave tortillas for 30 seconds each. Fill tortillas with steak mixture and roll. Garnish with sour cream and guacamole.

Makes 8 servings   Mild

Whole spices stay fresh for about 2 years while ground spices usually lasts 6 months. Dried herbs will keep their flavors for about a year.

Fiesta Skillet

1 pound ground beef
1 cup chopped onions
$1/2$ cup diced green pepper
$1^1/2$ cups water
1 cup rice, uncooked
1 teaspoon chili powder
$1/2$ teaspoon cumin
$1/2$ teaspoon seasoned salt
$1/2$ teaspoon pepper

In a large skillet over medium heat, brown beef, onion, and green pepper. Drain grease from meat mixture. Stir in remaining ingredients, bring to a boil. Reduce heat, cover and simmer for 20 minutes or until rice is tender.

Makes 6 servings   Medium

Mild Version: *Reduce chili powder to $1/4$ teaspoon chili powder and eliminate the cumin.*

Keep chile powder in the refrigerator to keep it from losing its flavor.

Chimichangas

1/2 pound ground beef
1/4 pound ground pork
1 clove garlic, minced
1/2 cup chopped onion
1 fresh Jalapeno pepper, seeded and minced
1 tablespoon cider vinegar
1 teaspoon chili powder
1 teaspoon brown sugar
1/4 teaspoon salt
1/4 teaspoon cumin
1/4 teaspoon oregano, crushed
1/2 cup canned tomatoes, drained
  and finely chopped
8 (12 inch) flour tortillas
1 cup refried beans
1 cup shredded Monterey Jack cheese
Vegetable oil for frying

Chimichanga translated is 'what chama calls it'.

In a large skillet brown beef and pork over medium high heat. Add garlic, onion, and Jalapeno pepper. Reduce heat to medium and cook until onion is tender. Drain grease and add vinegar, chili powder, brown sugar, salt, cumin, oregano, and tomatoes. Simmer 15 minutes, stirring constantly. In the center of each tortilla spoon 2 tablespoons of the refried beans, 2 tablespoons of cheese and 1/4 cup of meat mixture. Fold the tortilla over filling and fold in the ends. Secure with toothpicks. In a large skillet pour oil to an inch depth, heat over medium high heat. When oil is hot place filled tortilla seam down into oil. Add a second and cook 1 minute or until golden brown. Carefully turn over and cook the other side for 1 minute or until golden brown. Place on paper towel to drain. Repeat until all tortillas are cooked.

Makes 8 servings   Wild & Hot

Mild Version: Eliminate cumin and Jalapeno, reduce chili powder to 1/4 teaspoon.

Mexicano Pizza

Preheat oven to 350 degrees

1 pound ground beef
1 (1 ounce) package taco seasoning
1/2 cup water
2 prebaked pizza crusts
1 (16 ounce) can refried beans
3/4 cup salsa
2 cups crushed tortilla chips
2 cups shredded cheddar cheese
1 cup chopped lettuce
2 tomatoes, chopped

In a large skillet, brown ground beef, drain grease. Add taco seasoning and water, Simmer 5 minutes. Place pizza crusts on ungreased baking pans. Spread beans and salsa evenly over crust. Layer beef, chips, and cheese. Bake for 15 minutes or until the cheese is melted. Before serving top with lettuce and tomatoes.

Makes 8 servings   Mild

When cooking meat, add salt at the end of the cooking time to keep meat moist.

Salsa Chicken

4 boneless skinless chicken breasts
10 ounces thick and chunky salsa
1 (15 ounce) can black beans,
  drained and rinsed
1 (81/4 ounce) can whole kernel corn,
  drained
1/4 cup water
2 tablespoons minced cilantro

In a large skillet, brown chicken breast, over medium heat. Add remaining ingredients, reduce heat and simmer 10 minutes.

Makes 4 servings   Mild

Taco Salsa Chicken

Preheat oven to 350 degrees

**1 pound boneless and skinless
  chicken breasts
1 (1.25 ounce) package taco seasoning mix
1 cup salsa
1 cup grated Monterey Jack cheese**

Coat the chicken breasts with the taco seasoning and place them in a 9 x 13 inch baking dish. Spread salsa on top of each chicken breast, cover with foil and bake for 35 minutes. During the last 10 minutes, top each chicken breast with the grated cheese.

Makes 3 servings   Medium

Freeze cheese for about 20 minutes before grating to keep the shreds neater.

Berry Berry Salsa Chicken

Preheat oven to 350 degrees

**1 pint fresh strawberries, chopped
1 pint fresh blueberries
1/4 cup sugar
2 tablespoons finely chopped onion
1 tablespoon lemon juice
2 drops hot pepper sauce
1/2 teaspoon pepper
1/4 cup slivered and toasted almonds
8 chicken breasts**

In a medium bowl combine all ingredients except the almonds and chicken. Cover and refrigerate. Place chicken breast in a 9 x 13 inch baking dish cover and bake for 40 to 45 minutes or until fully cooked. Top each chicken breast with 1/2 cup of berry mixture, sprinkle with toasted almonds.

Makes 8 servings   Mild

Cheesy Chicken Bake

Preheat oven to 350 degrees

3 cups cooked and cubed chicken
2 tomatoes, chopped
1 (10 3/4 ounce) can
 Cream of Mushroom Soup
3/4 cup sour cream
3/4 cup salsa
1 (4 ounce) can chopped Jalapeno
 peppers, drained
1 tablespoon chili powder
12 (6 inch) corn tortillas,
 cut into 1 inch pieces
1 cup shredded cheddar cheese

In a large bowl combine chicken, tomatoes, soup, sour cream, salsa, Jalapeno peppers and chili powder. In an 8 x 8 inch baking dish layer half of the tortilla strips. Spoon half of the chicken mixture over tortilla strips. Repeat process. Top with shredded cheese. Bake for 35 minutes or until cheese is melted.

Makes 8 servings   Wild & Hot

Mild Version: Eliminate the Jalapeno peppers and decrease the chili powder to 1/4 teaspoon. Use mild salsa

Before you cut an onion, place it in the freezer for 10 minutes.

Polo Bake

Preheat Oven to 375 degrees

1 (16 ounce) jar salsa
1 (15.5 ounce) can black beans,
   drained and rinsed
2 tablespoons sliced Jalapeno peppers
2 tablespoons flour
1 tablespoon Mexican spice
1 pound chicken breasts, boneless
   and skinless

In a large bowl, combine all ingredients except the chicken, mix well. Spoon half of mixture into a 9 x 9 inch baking pan. Place chicken breast on top of mixture. Pour remaining ingredients over chicken breast. Bake for 30 minutes.

Makes 6 cups   Medium

If you do not use the whole onion, keep it fresh longer by leaving the skin on the unused portion.

Spicy Chicken and Stuffing Bake

Preheat oven to 375 degrees

1 (6 ounce) package stuffing mix
4 boneless cooked and shredded
  chicken breasts
1 (10^3/$_4$ ounce) can cream of
  chicken soup
^{1}/$_2$ cup sour cream
2 (4 ounce) cans diced green chiles

Prepare stuffing mix according to package directions, set aside. In a 13 x 9 inch baking pan, spread chicken evenly in bottom of the pan. In a small bowl combine soup, sour cream, and green chile, spoon over chicken. Sprinkle stuffing evenly over soup mixture. Bake for 45 minutes.

Makes 4 servings   Mild

Tortilla Chip Chicken

1 pound chicken breasts, cut into strips
1 tablespoon vegetable oil
1 (16 ounce) can corn, drained
1 (15 ounce) can tomato sauce
1 (4 ounce) can diced green chiles
1^1/$_2$ teaspoons chili powder
1 teaspoon onion powder
4 cups tortilla chips
1^1/$_2$ cups shredded cheddar cheese

In a large skillet over medium high heat, sauté chicken in vegetable oil until fully cooked. Stir in corn, tomato sauce, green chiles, chili powder, and onion powder. Place chicken on a bed of tortillas, top with cheese.

Makes 4 servings   Medium

Pick onions with tightly closed necks and have bright and shiny skin.

Raging Rigatoni

Preheat oven to 400 degrees

1 (16 ounce) box rigatoni noodles, cooked, drain
2 (16 ounce) jars Alfredo Sauce
1/2 cup milk, divided
1 pound chicken breasts, cooked, shredded
2 (4 ounce) cans diced green chiles
2 (8 ounce) packages mozzarella cheese

In a 4 quart baking dish, spread rigatoni noodles. Pour 1 1/2 jars of Alfredo sauce over noodles, mix well. Add 1/4 cup of milk to the empty jar and shake. Pour over noodles. Place chicken evenly over noodles. Pour remaining Alfredo sauce over chicken. Add remaining milk to jar and shake. Pour over chicken. Sprinkle green chiles evenly over Alfredo sauce. Sprinkle mozzarella cheese over top. Bake 45 minutes or until cheese is completely melted.

Makes 8 servings   Mild

Store onions in a cool dry place that allows air to circulate.

Taste of the West Chicken

Preheat oven to 350 degrees

8 chicken breasts
1 1/2 cups barbecue sauce
8 slices mozzarella cheese
1 (4 ounce) can diced green chiles
1 tomato, chopped

Place chicken breast in a 9 x 13 inch baking dish. Top each breast with barbecue sauce. Cover and bake 1 hour. Place a slice of cheese on each breast. Broil 1 to 2 minutes. Top with green chiles and tomatoes and serve.

Makes 8 servings   Mild

Nacho Crunch Chicken

Preheat oven to 375 degrees

1 (8 ounce) carton sour cream
2 teaspoons taco seasoning
4 chicken breasts, boneless and skinless
3 cups square cheese flavored
  crackers, crushed
1 cup butter or margarine, melted

In a medium bowl, combine sour cream and taco seasoning. Dredge chicken in sour cream mixture. Roll in cracker crumbs. Place in a baking dish. Pour melted butter over chicken. Bake 40 minutes.

Makes 4 servings   Mild

Spicy Stuffed Chicken Breast

6 chicken breasts, boneless and skinless
1 (7 ounce) can green chile strips
1 (8 ounce) package Monterey Jack
  cheese, cut in strips
1 egg, beaten
3 cups bread crumbs
1 tomato, chopped

Pound chicken breast until very thin. Place equal amounts of green chile strips and cheese on each chicken breast. Fold each edge over. Dip chicken in egg, roll in bread crumbs. Let stand for 5 minutes. In a large skillet over medium high heat, fry chicken in 1/2 inch of vegetable oil. Top with tomato and serve.

Makes 6 servings   Medium

A great way to store onions is by placing them in a clean pair of pantyhose, tie a knot between each onion. Just snip off an onion below the knot.

Over the Border Chicken

Preheat oven to 375 degrees

4 cups crushed Chex® corn cereal
1 (1.5 ounce) taco seasoning
6 chicken breasts, boneless and skinless
1/2 cup butter or margarine, melted

In a medium bowl, combine cereal and taco seasoning. Dip chicken breast in butter, roll in cereal mixture. Place in a 9 x 13 inch baking dish. Sprinkle remaining cereal mixture and butter over top of chicken breasts. Bake 35 to 45 minutes.

Makes 6 servings   Mild

Onions can be frozen up to 12 months.

Cilantro Chicken

6 chicken breasts, boneless and skinless
1/2 cup butter
1/4 cup vegetable oil
3 cloves garlic, minced
1/2 cup chopped cilantro
1/4 cup lemon juice
3 cups rice, cooked

Cut chicken into thin strips. In a large skillet over medium high heat, saute all ingredients until chicken is fully cooked. Serve on a bed of rice.

Makes 6 servings   Mild

Cordova Chicken

4 chicken breasts, boneless and skinless
Salt and pepper to taste
1 cup tomato and herb salad dressing
2 teaspoons Jalapeno pepper sauce

Season chicken with salt and pepper. In a large skillet over medium high heat, brown chicken breast. Add salad dressing and pepper sauce, cover and simmer 10 minutes.

Makes 4 servings   Wild & Hot

Mild Version: Eliminate Jalapeno pepper sauce. Add 1 tablespoon canned mild diced green chiles.

Chicken Con Queso

Preheat oven to 450 degrees

4 chicken breasts, boneless and skinless
2 (15 1/2 ounce) cans black beans,
  rinsed and drained
1/4 cup chopped with tops green onion
2 tablespoons minced cilantro
1 cup con queso cheese sauce
1/2 cup thick and chunky salsa
2 cups crushed coarsely, tortilla chips

Cut chicken into bite size pieces. Combine chicken, beans, onion, cilantro, cheese sauce, and salsa in a lightly greased 2 quart baking dish. Cover and bake for 30 minutes. Serve on a bed of crushed tortilla chips.

Makes 4 servings   Medium

 An onion a day can raise your HDL's or the good cholesterol, resulting in lower blood pressure..

Chimi Chicken

Preheat oven to 425 degrees

1/2 cup chopped onion
2 cloves garlic, minced
1 tablespoon olive oil
2 cups salsa
1 teaspoon chili powder
1/2 teaspoon cumin
2 chicken breasts, cooked and shredded
1 cup refried beans
6 (10 inch) flour tortillas
2 tablespoons vegetable oil

Cut onions under water to avoid tears.

In a large skillet over medium high heat, sauté onion and garlic in olive oil until tender. Stir in salsa, chili powder, cumin, and chicken. Reduce heat, simmer 20 minutes. Down the center of each tortilla, place an equal amount of refried beans. Spoon chicken mixture over beans. Fold up bottoms and sides of tortilla, secure with a toothpick. Place tortillas seam side down in a lightly greased 9 x 13 inch baking dish. Brush sides and top with vegetable oil. Bake for 15 minutes or until golden brown.

Makes 6 servings   Medium

Mild Version: Eliminate chili powder and cumin.

Chicken Enchiladas

Preheat oven to 350 degrees

4 chicken breasts, boneless,
  skinless and cubed
2 cups shredded cheddar cheese
1 cup sour cream
1 onion, chopped
1/2 teaspoon ground black pepper
1/2 teaspoon salt
1 (15 ounce) can tomato sauce
1 tablespoon chili powder
1 clove garlic, minced
1/3 cup green pepper, chopped
1/2 cup water
8 (10 inch) flour tortillas
1/2 cup salsa
3/4 cup shredded cheddar cheese

 Use clean cotton gloves when cutting onions to keep the smell off your hands.

In a large skillet over medium high heat, brown the chicken. Drain any grease from the pan. Add 2 cups cheddar cheese, sour cream, and black pepper. Heat over medium heat until the cheese melts. Add onion, pepper, salt, tomato sauce, chili powder, garlic, green pepper, and the water. Heat mixture, stirring often. Spoon equal amounts of mixture into the tortillas and roll. In a 9 x 13 inch pan, arrange the tortillas. Cover with salsa and cheddar cheese. Bake uncovered for 20 minutes.

Makes 8 servings   Medium

Mild Version: Use only a 1/4 teaspoon of chili powder and use mild salsa.

Chicken Enchilada Bake

Preheat oven to 350

1 cup chopped onion
1½ cups cooked shredded chicken breast
1 cup salsa
1 cup shredded cheddar cheese, divided
⅓ cup cream cheese
1 teaspoon cumin
8 (6 inch) flour tortillas
1½ cups taco sauce

Coat a large non stick skillet with cooking spray. Sauté onions over medium heat until tender. Add chicken, salsa, ½ cup cheese, cream cheese, and cumin. Cook until cheese melts. Spoon ⅓ cup of mixture down the center of each tortilla. Roll tortillas and place in a 9 x 13 inch baking pan. Drizzle taco sauce over top and sprinkle remaining cheese. Cover and bake for 15 minutes or until cheese melts.

Makes 8 servings   Mild

An easy way to get cheese off your grater is by grating a raw potato before you wash the grader.

Taco Chicken Bake

Preheat oven to 375 degrees

4 cups crushed square corn cereal
1 (1.25 ounce) package taco seasoning mix
6 boneless chicken breasts
½ cup butter or margarine, melted

In a medium bowl, combine cereal and taco seasoning, mix well. Place melted butter in a small bowl. Dip chicken breast in butter, then roll in cereal mixture until coated. Place chicken breast in a 13 x 9 inch baking dish. Combine left over cereal mixture and butter, sprinkle over top of chicken breast. Bake for 45 minutes.

Makes 6 servings   Mild

Chicken Tacos

1/3 cup pineapple juice
2 tablespoons soy sauce
1 tablespoon lemon juice
2 teaspoons taco seasoning
1/2 teaspoon Cayenne pepper
1/4 teaspoon garlic salt
12 ounces chicken breasts, cut into strips
8 hard corn taco shells
2 cups shredded cheddar cheese
1 cup salsa
1/2 cup diced onion
1 cup chopped lettuce
1 tomato, diced

In a large plastic bag, combine pineapple juice, soy sauce, lemon juice, taco seasoning, Cayenne pepper, and garlic salt. Add chicken strips and marinate in refrigerator for at least 1 hour, turning bag over after 10 minutes. Remove chicken and discard marinade. In a large skillet over medium heat, brown chicken. Microwave taco shells for 35 seconds or until warm. Place chicken down the center of each taco shell. Top with cheese, salsa, onion, lettuce, and tomato.

Makes 8 servings   Mild

 To keep the open edge of cheese from drying out, coat it with butter.

Chicken Fajitas

Preheat oven to 350 degrees

1 pound chicken breasts, cut into strips
1 tablespoon lime juice
1 teaspoon chili powder
1/2 teaspoon ground cumin
1/4 teaspoon salt
1/4 teaspoons pepper
4 (8 inch) flour tortillas
2/3 cup sliced with tops, green onions
1/2 cup sour cream
2 cups chopped lettuce
1 tomato, chopped

In a large skillet over medium heat, sauté chicken in lime juice with chili powder, cumin, salt, and pepper, until chicken is no longer pink in the middle. Wrap tortillas in a wet paper towel, microwave for 30 seconds. Divide chicken evenly between tortillas, top with onion, sour cream, lettuce, and tomato.

Makes 4 servings   Mild

The Mole is considered Mexico's national dish.

Salsa Chicken Wraps

2 cups cooked and cubed chicken
1 cup salsa
1 (11 ounce) can corn, drained
8 (6 inch) flour tortillas
1 cup shredded cheddar cheese

In a 2 quart saucepan over medium heat, combine chicken, salsa, and corn. Heat thoroughly. Heat tortillas in microwave for 20 seconds. On each heated tortilla place 1/2 cup of chicken mixture, sprinkle with cheese. Roll up and secure with a toothpicks.

Makes 8 wraps   Mild

The Mole

2½ pounds chicken pieces
2 tablespoons vegetable oil
1 clove garlic, chopped
1 cup chopped onion
1 cup chicken broth
2½ cups thick and chunky salsa
3 tablespoons creamy peanut butter
3 tablespoons chili powder
2 tablespoons cocoa powder

Heat oil in a large skillet over medium high heat. Add chicken pieces and brown on all sides. Remove from heat and set aside. In the same skillet, sauté garlic and onion until tender. Add remaining ingredients and bring to a boil. Reduce heat to medium low and add the chicken. Simmer uncovered for 25 minutes or until the chicken is fully cooked.

Makes 8 servings   Wild & Hot

Mild Version: Reduce chili powder to ½ teaspoon and use mild salsa

A Nun from the Convento de Santa Rosa de Puebla created the dish called 'Mole Poblano'. She first served it at a dinner to receive the new archbishop.

Dynamite Drumsticks

Preheat oven to 350 degrees

3/4 cup catsup
1/4 cup chile sauce
2 tablespoons vinegar
1 tablespoon brown sugar
1 teaspoon chili powder
1/4 teaspoon ground red pepper
1/4 teaspoon garlic powder
1/8 teaspoon dry mustard
8 chicken drumsticks

In a small saucepan over medium heat, combine all ingredients except drumsticks. Simmer for 10 minutes. Arrange drumsticks in a round 12 inch baking dish, with thickest part toward edge of dish so it looks like spokes on a wheel. Pour sauce over drumsticks, cover with tin foil and bake for 45 minutes or until chicken is no longer pink at the bone.

Makes 8 servings   Medium

Spread lemon juice over your chicken before baking to give it a golden color when baked.

Polo Pizza

Preheat oven to 400 degrees

1¹/₂ cups salsa
1 (12 inch) prepared pizza crust
2 chicken breasts, cooked and cut into
  bite sized pieces
¹/₂ cup sliced red pepper
¹/₄ cup chopped onion
2 cups shredded mozzarella
  and cheddar cheese
1 teaspoon minced cilantro

Spread salsa evenly onto pizza crust. Place chicken on salsa. Sprinkle red pepper and onion. Top with cheese. Sprinkle cilantro over cheese. Bake 15 minutes

Makes 6 servings   Mild

Sweet and Spicy Chicken

¹/₂ cup catsup
¹/₄ cup apricot preserves
2 ¹/₂ teaspoons Mexican seasoning
¹/₂ teaspoon chili powder
2 pounds cut up chicken pieces

In a small saucepan over medium heat, combine catsup, preserves, Mexican seasoning, and chili powder until preserves are melted. Cool slightly. In a 13 x 9 inch baking dish, arrange chicken in one layer. Pour sauce over chicken, coating all sides. Broil 6 inches from medium high heat 12 to 14 minutes, turning chicken to cook completely.

Makes 6 servings   Medium

Mild Version: *Reduce Mexican seasoning to 1 teaspoon. Eliminate the chili powder.*

Chiles will remain fresh longer if you remove the stems before storing.

Turkey Empanadas

Preheat oven to 350 degrees

1½ tablespoons olive oil
1 pound ground turkey
¼ cup diced bell pepper
2 cloves garlic, minced
½ teaspoon ground red pepper
¾ cup canned tomato, drained
2 tablespoons raisins
1 (8 ounce) can refrigerator biscuits

In a large non-stick skillet, heat oil over medium high heat. Add turkey and bell pepper, garlic, and red pepper. Cook until turkey is fully cooked. Add tomatoes and raisins, reduce heat and simmer for 20 minutes. Flatten each biscuit to a 4 inch round circle. Place ¼ cup of meat mixture on each biscuit, fold and wet edge with water, pinch edges to close. Place on a large baking sheet and bake for 15 minutes or until golden brown.

Makes 8 servings   Medium

Salsas are thicker and chunkier than picante sauces.

148

Sizzlin' Skillet

1 pound ground turkey
1 (15 1/2 ounce) can chili beans
1 1/2 cups cooked rice
1 cup salsa
1 tablespoons vinegar
3 teaspoons chili powder
1 teaspoon ground cumin
1 teaspoon sugar
1/2 teaspoon garlic salt
1/4 teaspoon pepper
1/4 cup shredded cheddar cheese

In a large skillet over medium high heat, brown turkey. Add beans, rice, salsa, vinegar, chili powder, cumin, sugar, garlic salt, and pepper. Bring to a boil. Reduce heat and simmer covered for 20 minutes. Sprinkle with cheese before serving.

Makes 5 servings   Wild & Hot

Mild Version: Reduce chili powder to 1/2 teaspoon.

 Release the flavor of dry herbs by crumbling them before adding to a recipe.

Turkey Tortillas

10 corn tortillas
20 slices turkey lunch meat
1 avocado, peeled, pitted, sliced
1/2 cup sour cream
1/2 cup shredded cheddar cheese
1/4 cup salsa

In a large skillet, heat corn tortillas till lightly browned. Place 2 slices of turkey on each tortilla. Top with avocado, sour cream, cheese, and salsa. Roll up and serve.

Makes 10 servings   Mild

Pueblo Pork Chops

4 thin cut pork chops
1 tablespoon vegetable oil
2 (16 ounce) cans baked beans
1 (15.25 ounce) can corn, drained
1/4 cup chopped onions
2 tablespoons chile sauce
1 teaspoon garlic salt

In a large skillet over medium high heat, brown pork chops in vegetable oil. Add remaining ingredients. Bring to a boil, reduce heat and simmer 20 minutes.

Makes 4 servings   Mild

 In 1810 the Mexican people revolted against the Spanish rule.

Cancun Chops

4 (3/4-inch) pork chops
1 (11 ounce) can Mexican style corn,
   not drained
1 cup chunky salsa

Spray a large skillet with nonstick spray. Over medium heat, cook pork chops until meat is no longer pink, remove to a platter. Add corn and salsa to pan. Cook for 3 minutes until hot. Spoon over pork chops.

Makes 4 servings   Medium

Mild Version: Use regular whole kernel corn instead of the Mexican style corn. Use mild salsa.

Cozemel Chops

6 boneless pork loin chops
1 tablespoon vegetable oil
1¹/₂ cups salsa
1 (4 ounce) can diced green chiles
1 teaspoon salt

In a large skillet, brown pork loin in vegetable oil. Add salsa, green chiles, and salt. Cover and simmer for 20 minutes.

Makes 6 servings   Medium

Ham and Cheese Tortillas

4 (12 inch) flour tortillas
¹/₂ cup cream cheese
1 (4 ounce) can diced green chiles
12 slices ham

Microwave tortillas for 30 second. Spread cream cheese on each tortilla. Sprinkle green chiles evenly on top of cream cheese. Place 3 slices of ham on each tortilla. Roll up and serve.

Makes 4 servings   Medium

Mexico's official Independence Day is September 16th.

Santa Fe Baked Fish

Preheat oven to 400 degrees

1½ pounds cod fillets
1 cup hot salsa
1 cup shredded cheddar cheese
½ cup crushed corn chips
¼ cup sour cream
1 avocado, sliced
¼ cup sliced black olives

Place fish fillets in an 8 x 12 inch greased baking dish. Cover with salsa and sprinkle cheddar cheese over each fillet. Top with crushed corn chips. Bake, uncovered for approximately 15 minutes or until fish flakes with a fork. Top each fillet with sour cream, avocado, and black olives.

Makes 6 servings   Medium

Mild Version: Substitute mild salsa for hot salsa.

The first Mexican peso coin was struck in 1866.

Southwestern Orange Roughy

4 orange roughy fillets, thawed
½ teaspoon cumin
½ teaspoon oregano
1 cup hot salsa

Sprinkle each side of each fillet with cumin and oregano. Place in a large non-stick skillet seasoned side down. Cook over medium heat for 3 minutes. Turn fillet over and top with salsa. Reduce heat; simmer for 6 minutes uncovered. Fillet is fully cooked when it flakes easily with fork.

Makes 4 servings   Wild & Hot

Mild Version: Substitute mild salsa for hot salsa.

Hacienda Halibut

Preheat oven to 350 degrees

1 (16 ounce) package frozen halibut fillets
2 tablespoons butter or margarine
1 (8 ounce) jar thick and chunky salsa
1 (2.2 ounce) can sliced black olives

Place frozen halibut in a 9 x 13 inch baking dish. Cover and bake 25 minutes. Pour butter then salsa over each fillet. Sprinkle black olives over salsa. Bake uncovered 15 minutes.

Makes 5 servings   Medium

Chile Pepper Catfish

Preheat oven to 350 degrees

1 cup diced and seeded tomato
1/2 cup chopped yellow bell pepper
1/2 cup chopped red bell pepper
2 tablespoons minced cilantro
2 tablespoons canned diced green chiles
1 tablespoon minced onion
1/4 teaspoon salt
1/4 teaspoon pepper
1 tablespoon balsamic vinegar
3 tablespoons lime juice, divided
4 (4 ounce) catfish fillets

In a medium bowl, combine tomato, bell peppers, cilantro, green chiles, onion, salt, pepper, vinegar, and 2 tablespoons lime juice, let stand 1 hour. Place fish fillets in a 7 x 11 inch baking dish. Sprinkle remaining 1 tablespoon lime juice over fish. Cover dish with tin foil and bake for 30 to 35 minutes or until fish flakes easily. Pour bell pepper mixture over fish. Heat in oven for 2 minutes.

Makes 4 servings   Mild

To get the garlic smell off your hands, rub with lemon juice and salt, rinse under cold water.

Spanish Spinach Enchiladas

Preheat oven to 350 degrees

1 (10 ounce) package frozen spinach, thawed and drained
1 (10 3/4 ounce) can cream of chicken soup
1 cup sour cream
1 (3 ounce) can Jalapeno peppers
1/2 clove garlic, minced
8 (8 inch) flour tortillas
1 1/2 cups shredded Monterey Jack cheese
6 green onions, chopped with tops

In a blender, puree spinach, soup, sour cream, Jalapeno peppers, and garlic. Pour enough spinach mixture in a 9 x 13 inch baking pan, to coat bottom. On each tortilla, spread evenly Monterey Jack cheese and green onions. Roll up tortillas and place in baking pan. Pour remaining spinach mixture over tortillas. Bake for 25 minutes.

Makes 8 servings   Medium

Garlic breath: Chew on 3 or 4 sprigs of parsley or suck on a lemon wedge.

Easy Enchiladas

10 (10 inch) flour tortillas
1 cup shredded cheddar cheese
1 onion, chopped
1 (15 ounce) can enchilada sauce

On each tortilla, sprinkle cheese and onion. Roll tortilla and place seam side down in a microwave safe dish. Microwave 1 1/2 minutes on high. Cover with enchilada sauce, microwave an additional 45 seconds.

Makes 10 servings   Mild

Cheese Enchiladas

Preheat oven to 350 degrees

1 (8 ounce) package cream cheese,
   softened
1 (8 ounce) package shredded
   cheddar cheese
1/4 cup sliced with tops green onion
6 (8 inch) flour tortillas
1 (16 ounce) jar salsa

In a medium bowl, combine cream cheese,
1 cup cheddar cheese, and onions, mix well.
Spread an even amount of cheese mixture
down the center of each tortilla. Roll up and
place seam side down in a 7 x 11 inch baking
dish. Pour salsa over tortillas. Top with
remaining cheddar cheese. Bake 25 minutes.

Makes 6 servings   Mild

Storing
cheese in
a tightly
covered container
with a few cubes
of sugar will
keep it from
molding as
quickly.

Chiles Rellenos

8 large Pablano peppers, roasted and peeled
1/2 pound Monterey Jack cheese,
   cut into 1/2 x 3 inch strips
1/2 cup flour
1/2 teaspoon baking powder
1/4 teaspoon baking soda
1/4 teaspoon salt
1/2 cup buttermilk
1 egg

Slit chiles from stem to tip. Insert cheese strip in each pepper. In a medium bowl, combine flour, baking powder, baking soda, and salt. In a small bowl, mix buttermilk and egg. Add egg mixture to flour mixture, mix well; the batter should be the same consistency as pancake batter, add water if too thick. Dip each pepper in batter. Deep fry each pepper. Top with green or red chile sauce and cheese if desired.

Makes 4 servings   Mild

Add a few grains of rice to your salt shaker to keep it from clogging.

Nacho Supreme Meal

1 (30 ounce) can chili with beans
1 (10 3/4 ounce) can nacho cheese soup
3/4 cup milk
1 (12 ounce) package tortilla chips, crushed
1/4 cup chopped with tops green onions
1/4 cup sour cream
1/4 cup sliced black olives, optional

In a large saucepan over medium heat, combine chili, nacho cheese soup, and milk, simmer 10 minutes. Place tortillas in the bottom of individual bowls. Pour chili mixture over tortillas. Top with onions, sour cream, and black olives and serve.

Makes 6 servings   Mild

Black Bean Burritos

Bake at 350 degrees

3/4 pound pork sausage
1/2 cup chopped green pepper
1/3 cup chopped onion
1 1/2 cups salsa, divided
1 1/2 cups cooked long grain rice
1 (15 ounce) can black beans,
   drained and rinsed
1 cup shredded cheddar cheese, divided
10 (7 inch) flour tortillas

In a large skillet over medium high heat, brown sausage, pepper, and onion; drain. Stir in 1 cup salsa, rice, and beans, mix well. In the center of each tortilla spread 1/2 cup sausage mixture down the center, sprinkle 1 tablespoon of cheese over mixture. Roll up and place seam down in a greased 13 x 9 inch baking pan. Spread remaining salsa over tortillas. Cover and bake for 30 minutes. Uncover and sprinkle with remaining cheese. Bake for 10 minutes longer.

Make 10 servings   Medium

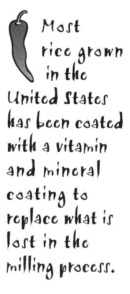

Most rice grown in the United States has been coated with a vitamin and mineral coating to replace what is lost in the milling process.

Jalapeno Cheese Soufflé

Preheat oven to 325 degrees

4 tablespoons butter
1/4 cup flour
1 1/4 cups milk
2 cups (8 ounces) shredded Monterey Jack cheese with Jalapenos
5 large eggs, yolks separated from whites
1 large egg white

An easy way to separate eggs is by breaking them into a funnel. The whites will slip through and the yolk will remain in the funnel.

Melt butter in a 2-quart saucepan over medium heat. Stir in flour until well blended; cook 1 minute stirring constantly. Gradually add milk, stirring often until mixture boils. Cook an additional 2 minutes stirring constantly. Remove from heat, add cheese, stir until melted.

In a large bowl, whisk egg yolks slightly. Gradually add cheese mixture to egg yolks, stirring constantly to prevent lumping and to make a smooth mixture. Cool 10 minutes.

In another large bowl, beat all 6 egg whites with a mixer at high speed, until stiff peaks form. With a rubber spatula, gently fold 1/4 of egg whites into the yolk mixture at a time. Mix until just blended. Do not over mix.

Pour into a soufflé dish. With the back of a spoon, 1 inch from the side of the soufflé dish, make a 1 inch indentation all the way around the dish, causing the center to raise higher then the edge.

Bake for 55 to 60 minutes or until a knife inserted under to crust comes out wet but clean.

Makes 6 servings   Medium

On the Edge

Vegetables, Pasta, Rice & Casseroles

Santa Fe Baked Potato

Preheat oven to 400 degrees

4 large baking potatoes
2 cups cooked and cubed chicken
1 cup whole kernel corn, drained
1 cup salsa
1 cup shredded cheddar cheese

Bake potatoes for 55 minutes or until tender. In a large skillet over medium heat, add chicken, corn, and salsa, cook for 3 minutes. Cut potatoes lengthwise, remove all but 1/4 inch of potato from the inside, leaving a shell. Place scooped out potato in a medium bowl. Add chicken mixture and mix together. Refill potato shell with combined mixture. Top with cheddar cheese and bake for 15 minutes.

Makes 4 servings   Mild

Cumin is a common spice in Indian, Mexican, Latin American, Asian, African, and Middle Eastern cuisine.

Tex-Mex Tator

1 pound ground beef
1 cup salsa
1 tablespoon chili powder
4 potatoes, cooked and split
1/2 cup shredded cheddar cheese

In a large skillet over medium high heat, brown beef. Drain grease. Stir in salsa and chili powder, heat. Spoon beef mixture over fluffed potato. Top with cheese. Microwave 30 seconds to melt cheese.

Makes 4 servings   Medium

Mild Version: *Reduce or eliminate chili powder.*

Stuffed Baked Potatoes

Preheat oven to 350 degrees

4 medium potatoes
1/2 cup diced cooked ham
1/2 cup sour cream
3 tablespoons grated Parmesan cheese
2 tablespoons mayonnaise
2 tablespoons chopped green chiles
1 cup shredded cheddar cheese

Place potatoes in a 13 x 9 inch baking dish. Cut a X on top of each potato. Bake uncovered for 60 minutes. In a medium bowl combine ham, sour cream, Parmesan cheese, mayonnaise, and green chiles. With a fork, fluff potato pulp. Top each potato with the ham mixture, sprinkle with cheddar cheese. Bake an additional 15 minutes

Makes 4 servings   Medium

Mild Version: Reduce green chiles to 2 teaspoons.

Paprika is a milder form of red pepper.

Queso Potatoes

1 (10 3/4 ounce) can condensed cheddar cheese soup
1/2 cup salsa
1 teaspoon garlic salt
4 cups cooked and cubed potatoes

In a large skillet over medium heat, combine soup, salsa, and garlic salt, heat. Stir in potatoes, simmer 10 minutes over low heat. Garnish with additional salsa.

Makes 8 servings   Mild

Spicy Potato Skins

Preheat oven to 400 degrees

6 large baking potatoes
1/4 cup butter or margarine
1/2 teaspoon hot pepper sauce
1/2 teaspoon chili powder
6 slices bacon, cooked and crumbled
1/4 cup chopped with tops green onion
1 1/2 cups shredded
**   Monterey Jack cheese**
1 cup sour cream

Clean and dry potatoes. Bake 1 hour or until tender. Or you can microwave the potatoes until tender. Cut each potato in half. Scoop out the insides, leaving only 1/4 to 1/2 inch of potato on each skin. Cut each potato skin in 1/3 strips. Place skins on a baking sheet and broil 4 inches from heat for 4 minutes. In a small bowl combine butter, hot pepper sauce, and chili powder. Brush butter mixture on each potato skin. Sprinkle bacon, onion, and cheese over buttered skin. Broil an additional 1 minute or until cheese has melted. Serve with sour cream.

Makes 6 servings   Medium

Speed up potato baking by soaking potatoes in hot water for 15 minutes, cut off the ends before baking.

Puerto Vallarta Potatoes

Preheat oven to 350 degrees

8 medium potatoes, peeled and cubed
1 (10³/₄ ounce) condensed cream
  of chicken soup
3 cups shredded cheddar cheese, divided
1 cup sour cream
1 (4 ounce) can diced green chiles
3 green onions, chopped
¹/₂ teaspoon salt

In a large saucepan, cover potatoes with water. Bring to a boil, cover and cook until tender. Drain, set aside. In a large bowl, combine soup, 1¹/₂ cups cheese, sour cream, green chiles, onion, and salt. Fold in potatoes. Pour potatoes into a lightly greased 13 x 9 inch baking dish. Top with remaining cheese. Bake for 30 minutes.

Makes 10 servings   Mild

To keep potatoes from growing buds as quickly, place an apple in the bag.

Pueblo Fried Potatoes

2 tablespoons butter
1 (5.5 ounce) package frozen
 hashbrowns
1/2 cup chopped onion
1/2 cup chopped green bell pepper
1/2 cup chopped red bell pepper
1 (4 ounce) can diced green chiles, drained
1 cup shredded cheddar cheese
1/2 teaspoon Cajun seasoning

In a large skillet melt butter. Combine all
ingredients except the cheddar cheese. Brown
over medium high heat. When potatoes are
browned, reduce heat and sprinkle the cheese
over top of mixture. Cover until the cheese
is melted.

Serves 6   Medium

*Mild Version: Eliminate the green chiles and
Cajun seasoning.*

Cut the potato baking time in half by boiling for 10 minutes before you bake.

Chile Cream Corn

1 (10 ounce) package frozen whole
 kernel corn
1/4 cup chopped red bell pepper
1/4 cup green chopped bell pepper
1/2 cup water
1/4 cup cream cheese, softened
1 (4 ounce) can diced green chiles
1 tablespoon milk
1/4 teaspoon salt

In a large saucepan over medium heat,
combine corn, peppers, and water. Simmer
10 minutes. Drain water. Add cream cheese,
chiles, milk, and salt. Simmer 5 minutes,
stirring frequently.

Makes 6 servings   Mild

Mexi Corn Bake

Preheat oven to 325 degrees

2 (8 ounce) packages cream cheese
1/2 cup butter
4 (14.25 ounce) cans corn, drained
1 (4 ounce) can chopped green chiles

In a medium saucepan melt cream cheese and butter over low heat. Add corn and chiles. Mix well. Pour into an 8 x 8 inch baking dish. Bake for 30 minutes.

Serves 8   Medium

Chile Powder has four main ingredients, cumin, Ancho chiles, garlic, and oregano.

San Carlos Squash

2 tablespoons olive oil
3 yellow squash, grated
1 onion, chopped

Heat oil in a large skillet over medium heat. Add squash and onions, cook for 5 minutes. Reduce heat, cook an additional 30 minutes. Stir occasionally.

Makes 4 servings   Mild

Santa Barbara Baked Squash

Preheat oven to 350 degrees

1 acorn squash, cut in half and seeded
2 tablespoons butter or margarine
2 tablespoons brown sugar
1/4 teaspoon salt

Place squash cut side up, in a 9 x 13 inch baking dish. Pour water to 1/4 inch in pan around squash. Cover and bake 30 minutes. In a small bowl, combine butter, sugar, and salt. Spread butter mixtures over each squash. Bake uncovered, an additional 20 minutes.

Makes 2 servings   Mild

Grande Green Beans

2 (16 ounce) cans green beans, drained
1 (16 ounce) can tomato and chiles
1 onion, chopped
2 slices bacon, fried crisp

In a large saucepan, combine green beans and tomato and chiles. Add onion and crumbled bacon. Bring to a boil. Reduce heat and simmer 10 minutes.

Makes 6 servings   Medium

Belen Broccoli and Chiles

Preheat oven to 350 degrees

1½ pounds fresh broccoli
2 Anaheim chiles, seeded and chopped
2 tablespoons butter or margarine, melted
½ teaspoon salt

Place broccoli and chiles in a 9 x 9 inch baking pan. Pour melted butter over top of broccoli. Sprinkle with salt. Bake for 15 minutes.

Makes 6 servings   Mild

Fresh broccoli will stay fresh up to 5 days in the refrigerator.

Odessa Onions

12 small white onions, chopped
2 (4 ounce) cans diced green chiles
5 tablespoons butter or margarine
2 tablespoons sugar

In a large skillet over medium heat, sauté onions and green chiles in butter. Add sugar after sauteing for 2 minutes. Cook until onion is tender. Serve over steak, chicken, or pork.

Makes 8 servings   Medium

Mild Version: *Use 1 tablespoon of green chiles instead of 2 cans.*

Bixby Banana Peppers

6 banana peppers, seeded
1¹/₂ cups cold water
1 cup cold milk
1 cup flour

Soak peppers in cold water for 10 minutes. Transfer peppers to cold milk, soak an additional 10 minutes. Roll peppers in flour. Dip in milk then roll in flour again. Deep fry in 360 degrees oil until golden brown. Drain on paper towel.

Makes 6 servings   Medium

Spanish Stuffed Peppers

Preheat oven to 350 degrees

3 green bell peppers
1 pound ground beef, browned
   and drained
1 (15 ounce) can Spanish rice
2 tablespoons catsup

Cut peppers in half, remove pulp. Steam peppers in 1 inch of water for 5 minutes. Cool. Combine beef, rice, and catsup. Spoon mixture into peppers. Place in a 8 x 8 inch baking dish. Bake 25 minutes.

Makes 6 servings   Mild

White and black pepper come from the same berry. White pepper is made from a ripe berry and black pepper is from an under ripe berry.

Mexican Vegetables

1 onion, chopped
1 green pepper, chopped
$1/2$ tablespoon vegetable oil
2 (15 ounce) cans hominy
2 ($14^1/2$ ounce) cans tomatoes, chopped
1 (4 ounce) can diced green chiles,
   drained
$1/4$ teaspoon chili powder
$1/4$ teaspoon garlic powder
$1/2$ tablespoon vegetable oil

In a large skillet, sauté onion and green
pepper in $1/2$ tablespoon of oil over medium
high heat, until tender. Add remaining
ingredients. Simmer for 20 minutes over
medium low heat.

Makes 8 servings   Medium

Mild Version: Eliminate green chiles.

Once
you open
a can do
not use it to
store unused
food.

Pinto Baked Beans

2 (15 ounce) cans pinto beans, drained
1 cup salsa
$1/4$ cup barbecue sauce
$1/4$ cup brown sugar
1 teaspoon cumin
$1/4$ teaspoon chili powder
4 slices bacon, cooked and crumbled

In a medium saucepan, combine all
ingredients. Bring to a boil. Reduce heat
and simmer 10 minutes.

Makes 6 servings   Medium

Santa Fe Beans

1 (15 ½ ounce) can kidney beans, drained
1 (15 ¼ ounce) can whole kernel corn,
  drained
1½ cups thick and chunky salsa
½ cup chopped green bell pepper
½ teaspoon chili powder

In a large saucepan, combine all ingredients.
Heat over medium heat for 5 minutes

Makes 6 servings   Medium

Taste a bean to check if it is done. If it is firm yet tender and does not taste of raw starch then it is done.

Frijoles Refritos

(Refried Beans)

1⅓ cups dried pinto beans
4½ cups water
⅓ cup plus 1 tablespoon shortening
1½ teaspoons salt
1 small onion, finely chopped
1 clove garlic, minced

In a 3 quart saucepan, combine beans, water, salt, onion, garlic, and 1 tablespoon of shortening. Heat on high until boiling; reduce heat to low, cover with a lid. Simmer. Add remaining shortening. Mix well. Mash beans to desired consistency.

Makes 6 servings   Mild

Easy Refried Beans

4 tablespoons bacon drippings
2 (15 ounce) cans pinto beans, mashed
1 clove garlic, finely minced
1 onion, finely minced
1/4 teaspoon salt
1/4 cup shredded Monterey Jack cheese

In a large skillet, heat bacon drippings over low heat. Add mashed beans, garlic, onion, and salt. Increase heat to medium and cook for 30 minutes. Top with Monterey Jack cheese.

Makes 6 servings   Mild

Black Bean Pasta

Preheat oven to 350 degree

1 (7 ounce) package elbow macaroni
1 (15 ounce) can black beans,
   drained and rinsed
1 (10 3/4 ounce) can nacho cheese soup
1/3 cup milk
1/2 cup crushed tortilla chips
1/2 cup shredded cheddar cheese
1/4 cup chopped black olives, optional

Prepare macaroni according to package. In a large bowl, combine macaroni and beans. Add soup and milk, mix well. Pour mixture into a greased 8 x 8 inch pan. Cover and bake for 25 minutes. Uncover, sprinkle tortilla chips, cheese, and olives over top. Bake an additional 10 minutes or until cheese is melted.

Makes 4 servings   Mild

Non-egg pasta can be stored up to 3 years. Egg pasta up to 2 years.

Mexican Lasagna

Preheat oven to 375 degrees

16 ounces lasagna noodles
1 pound ground beef
1 (1 ounce) package taco seasoning mix
1/2 cup water
1 (28 ounce) can tomato sauce
8 cups shredded cheddar cheese
1/2 cup crushed tortilla chips

Cook lasagna noodles, drain and set aside. In a large skillet, brown beef over medium heat, drain grease. Add taco seasoning, water and tomato sauce. Reduce and simmer for 5 minutes. In a 9 X 13 inch baking dish, layer noodles, meat mixture, and cheese: repeat until all ingredients are used. Bake for 30 minutes. Top with crushed tortilla chips before serving.

Serves 8   Mild

Peel tomatoes easier by placing them in boiling water for a few seconds.

San Pedro Chicken and Pasta

3 cups dry corkscrew macaroni,
  cooked and drained
2 cups frozen broccoli
1 red pepper, seeded and chopped
1 (10 3/4 ounce) can condensed cream
  of mushroom soup
1 1/2 cups cooked and cubed chicken
3/4 cup salsa
1/4 cup milk

In a large saucepan combine all ingredients. Simmer 15 minutes, stirring occasionally.

Makes 4 servings   Mild

Pablano Chile Pasta

1 pound linguine
1 fresh pablano chile, seeded
1 onion, chopped
1 clove garlic, minced
1½ cups heavy whipping cream
2 tablespoons butter
¼ pound shredded mozzarella cheese
   salt and pepper to taste

In a large pot bring to boil 4 quarts of water. Add linguine and pablano chile. When linguine is tender drain and remove the pablano chile. In a blender, puree together pablano chile, onion, garlic, and cream. In a large saucepan over medium heat, melt butter. Add the pureed mixture and salt and pepper to taste. Simmer 5 minutes. Stir in pasta and mozzarella cheese. Simmer for 10 minutes.

Serves 6   Medium

Chili Spaghetti

1 (4 ounce) package spaghetti
1 (15 ounce) can no bean chili
1 cup grated cheddar cheese

Cook and drain spaghetti. Set aside and keep warm. In a medium saucepan, add chili, heat over medium heat. Pour sauce over spaghetti. Top with cheddar cheese.

Makes 4 servings   Mild

Chop more onions and green peppers than is needed for your recipe. Store the extra in the freezer to be added to soups and casseroles.

San Salvador Chicken Spaghetti

1 pound chicken breasts, cut into cubes
1 Jalapeno pepper, seeded and chopped
1 tablespoon vegetable oil
1/4 teaspoon garlic powder
2 cups spaghetti sauce
1 (4 ounce) can sliced mushrooms, drained
8 ounces spaghetti, cooked and drained

In a large skillet over medium heat, sauté chicken, Jalapeno pepper, and garlic powder in oil, until chicken is no longer pink. Stir in spaghetti sauce and mushrooms. Bring to a boil. Reduce heat and simmer for 15 minutes. Serve over a bed of warm spaghetti noodles.

Makes 4 servings   Medium

Mild Version: Eliminate Jalapeno. Add a 4 ounce can of diced green chiles if a slightly spicy flavor is desired.

Store tomatoes at room temperature with the stems down.

Sedona Shrimp Pasta

2 small green peppers, cut in strips
1 cup sliced mushrooms
2 cloves garlic, minced
1 tablespoon vegetable oil
1 cup salsa
2 tomatoes, chopped
1 pound shrimp, peeled and deveined
3 1/4 cups macaroni, cooked and drained

In a large skillet over medium heat, sauté peppers, mushrooms, and garlic in vegetable oil until tender. Stir in salsa, tomato, and shrimp. Bring to a boil. Reduce heat and simmer for 10 minutes. Add macaroni, heat and serve.

Makes 4 servings   Mild

Baked Spanish Spaghetti

Preheat oven to 350 degrees

1 pound ground beef
1 cup spaghetti sauce
1 cup salsa
3 cups spaghetti, cooked and drained
1/3 cup grated Parmesan cheese
1 egg
1 tablespoon butter or margarine
1 cup cottage cheese
1 cup shredded mozzarella cheese

In a large skillet over medium high heat, brown beef. Drain grease. Stir in spaghetti sauce and salsa, heat. In a medium bowl, combine spaghetti, Parmesan cheese, egg, and butter. In a lightly greased 10 inch pie pan, spread spaghetti mixture on bottom and up sides. Spread cottage cheese over spaghetti. Top with beef mixture. Bake for 30 minutes. Top with mozzarella cheese and bake an additional 5 minutes.

Makes 6 servings   Mild

If you have a small grease fire on the stove, turn off stove and douse it with baking soda.

Fiery Fettuccine

1/2 cup salsa
1/2 cup sour cream
1/3 cup grated Parmesan cheese
1/2 teaspoon hot pepper sauce
1/4 teaspoon garlic salt
4 cups fettuccine, cooked and drained

In a large saucepan over medium heat, combine salsa, sour cream, Parmesan cheese, hot pepper sauce, and garlic salt. Simmer 10 minutes. Toss with fettuccine and serve.

Makes 4 servings   Medium

Mexican Manicotti

Preheat oven to 350 degrees

1 pound ground beef
1 (1.25 ounce) package taco seasoning
1 (8 ounce) package manicotti shells,
  cooked and drained
1 (16 ounce) jar salsa
2 cups shredded cheddar cheese
1 cup sour cream

In a large skillet brown beef. Drain grease. Add taco seasoning and prepare according to package directions. Stuff manicotti shells with taco meat, place in a lightly greased 9 x 13 inch baking dish. Pour salsa over shells. Top with cheese. Bake for 15 minutes or until cheese is melted. Serve with sour cream.

Makes 6 servings   Mild

Easy Mexi Mac

1 pound ground beef
1 (14½ ounce) can tomatoes, chopped
1 cup corn
1 cup salsa
1 tablespoon chili powder
3 cups elbow macaroni, cooked
½ cup shredded cheddar cheese

In a large skillet over medium high heat, brown beef. Drain grease. Add tomatoes, corn, salsa, and chili powder, bring to a boil. Reduce heat and simmer 10 minutes. Stir in macaroni. Sprinkle cheese on top and heat 2 minutes.

Makes 4 servings   Medium

When frying foods, spray the spatula with non-stick spray to keep food from sticking to it.

Mexi Mac

1 pound ground beef
1/2 cup chopped green bell pepper
1/2 cup chopped onion
3 cloves garlic, minced
2 cups elbow macaroni,
  cooked and drained
1/2 cup water
1 tablespoon chili powder
1 teaspoon ground cumin
1/2 teaspoon salt
1/4 teaspoon pepper
1 (14 1/2 ounce) can tomatoes, chopped
1 (15 ounce) can kidney beans, drained
1 (8 3/4 ounce) can whole kernel corn,
  drained
1 (8 ounce) can tomato sauce
1 (6 ounce) can tomato paste
1 cup shredded cheddar cheese

In a large skillet, brown beef, pepper, and onion. Drain grease. Add remaining ingredients, except cheese to beef mixture, stir well. Bring to a boil. Reduce heat, cover and simmer 20 minutes. Top with cheese and serve.

Make 8 servings   Mild

 To keep the non-stick finish from scratching when stored, place paper towel between pots.

Nacho Mac and Cheese

1½ pounds ground beef
¼ cup chopped onion
2 (7.25 ounces) package macaroni
   and cheese
1 cup extra hot salsa
1 (15 ounce) jar nacho cheese dip
1 (7 ounce) can diced green chiles

Brown beef and onion over medium heat.
Drain grease. In a large saucepan cook and
prepare macaroni and cheese according to
package directions. Stir in meat mixture, salsa,
nacho cheese dip, and green chiles. Reduce
heat and simmer 10 minutes or until heated
through out.

Serves 6   Wild & Hot

*Mild Version: Replace extra hot salsa with mild
hot sauce and the nacho cheese with regular
cheese dip.*

Store pasta
in a sealed
carton;
store in a cool
dry place.

Sweet and Spicy Mac and Cheese

1 (7 ounce) package elbow macaroni
1 (8 ounce) jar nacho cheese dip
1½ cups ham, cooked and cubed
1 (8 ounce) can crushed pineapple,
   drained
½ cup chopped green pepper
¼ cup chopped onions

Cook macaroni according to package,
drain. Stir in cheese dip, ham, pineapple,
pepper, and onions, stir well. Heat for 5
minutes or until warm.

Makes 4 servings   Mild

Taco Shells and Cheese

1 (24 ounce) box shells and cheese mix
1/2 pound pork sausage,
    cooked and drained
1/3 cup salsa
1 tablespoon taco seasoning
4 cups chopped lettuce
2 tomatoes, chopped
1/4 cup chopped onion
1 cup shredded cheddar cheese

Prepare shells and cheese according to package. Stir in sausage, salsa, and taco seasoning. Simmer over medium heat for 5 minutes. Place on a platter, top with lettuce, tomatoes, onion, and cheese.

Makes 6 servings   Medium

Chile Rice

Preheat oven to 350

1 cup cooked rice
8 ounces sour cream
1 cup diced green chiles,
    drained if using canned
1 cup shredded mozzarella cheese
1 cup shredded Monterey Jack cheese

In a large bowl, combine all ingredients together. Place into a greased 8 x 8 inch baking pan. Bake for 35 minutes.

Makes 6 servings   Medium

Mild Version: Use ¼ cup mild green chiles.

Romaine lettuce is not only greener than iceberg lettuce; it also has about 3 times as much vitamin C and about 6 times as much vitamin A.

Spicy Spanish Rice

Preheat oven to 400 degrees

1 cup rice, uncooked
1 onion, chopped
2 cloves garlic, minced
1 (10 3/4 ounce) can chicken broth
1 (14 1/2 ounce) can tomatoes with
  green chile
1 cup mixed peas and carrots

In a large skillet, over medium high heat, brown rice, onion, and garlic. When the rice is a light brown, add chicken broth and the can of tomatoes with green chiles. Cover and let simmer for 10 minutes. Add peas and carrots, mix well. Place mixture into an 8 x 8 inch baking pan. Bake for 1 hour.

Makes 6 servings   Medium

Milled white rice keeps almost indefinitely on the shelf. Store open rice in a tightly covered container.

Texas Beans and Rice

1 cup chopped onion
1 clove garlic, minced
1/2 teaspoon olive oil
1 cup cooked rice
1 (15 ounce) can pinto beans,
  drained and rinsed
1 (8 ounce) jar salsa
1 (4 ounce) can green chiles, diced
1/2 cup water
1 teaspoon chili powder
1/2 teaspoon hot pepper sauce

In a large skillet over medium heat, sauté onion and garlic in olive oil until tender. Add remaining ingredients. Bring to a boil. Reduce heat and simmer 10 minutes.

Makes 6 servings   Medium

Baked Jalapeno Rice

Preheat oven to 350 degrees

3 cups cooked rice
3 Jalapeno peppers, seeded and chopped
1 cup sour cream
1 cup shredded Monterey Jack cheese,
** divided**
1 cup corn
1/3 cup chopped green onions
2 tablespoons minced cilantro

In a large bowl, combine all ingredients except 1/4 cup Monterey Jack cheese. Mix well. pour mixture into a 9 x 9 inch baking dish. Bake 30 minutes. Sprinkle remaining 1/4 cup cheese on top of mixture, bake an additional 2 minutes.

Make 6 servings   Wild & Hot

 Leftover rice can be refrigerated for up to 4 days or frozen for 6 months.

Queso Rice

Preheat oven to 350 degrees

2 1/2 cups rice, cooked
1 (7 ounce) can diced green chiles
2 cups sour cream
1 cup shredded cheddar cheese

In a large bowl, combine all ingredients. Pour into a buttered 9 x 9 inch baking dish. Bake 35 minutes.

Makes 4 servings   Medium

Poza Rica Rice

1/2 cup diced onion
2 tablespoons vegetable oil
1 cup rice, uncooked
1/2 cup tomato sauce
13/4 cup chicken broth
1/4 teaspoon salt

In a large saucepan, sauté onions in oil until tender, over medium high heat. Add rice and lightly brown. Add tomato sauce, chicken broth, and salt. Bring to a boil. Reduce heat, cover and simmer 20 minutes.

Makes 6 servings   Mild

To keep rice white when cooking in hard water, add 1 teaspoon of lemon juice or 1 tablespoon vinegar to cooking water

Chile Relleno Bake

Preheat oven to 350 degrees

1 (21 ounce) can whole green chiles, drained
6 ounces cheddar cheese, shredded
4 eggs
1 1/2 cups milk
1/4 cup flour
1/2 teaspoon salt
1/4 teaspoon pepper

In a lightly greased 13 x 9 inch baking dish, line chiles across bottom. Sprinkle cheese over chiles. In a small bowl, combine eggs, milk, flour, salt, and pepper, mix well. Pour egg mixture gently over cheese. Bake for 30 minutes or until firm.

Makes 8 servings   Mild

Chile Relleno Casserole

Preheat oven to 350 degrees

**3 (4 ounce) cans whole green chiles,
   drained**
2 cups shredded Monterey Jack cheese
9 (8 inch) flour tortillas
2 (10 ounce) cans enchilada sauce
1 cup sour cream

Split each chile lengthwise into halves.
Arrange 2 chile halves and about 3$1/2$
tablespoons of cheese in the center of each
tortilla. Roll to enclose the filling. Arrange
seam down in a greased 9 x 13 inch baking
pan. Mix enchilada sauce and sour cream in
a small mixing bowl, spoon over rellenos.
Bake at 350 degrees for 30 minutes.

Makes 6 servings   Wild & Hot

Mild Version: Use 3 cans of mild green chiles

For more
flavorful
rice,
substitute
chicken broth
for the water.

Beef Enchilada Casserole

Preheat oven to 350 degrees

1 pound ground beef
12 (8 inch) corn tortillas
1 (14$1/2$ ounce) can enchilada sauce
**1 (16 ounce) package cheddar cheese,
   shredded**

In a large skillet over medium high heat
brown meat. Drain grease. In a 13 x 9 inch
baking dish, line the bottom of pan with 6
tortillas. Spread meat over tortillas. Spoon
half of enchilada sauce over meat. Top with
remaining tortillas. Spread remaining
enchilada sauce over tortillas. Sprinkle cheese
over enchilada sauce. Bake for 30 minutes.

Makes 6 servings   Mild

Chicken Enchilada Casserole

Preheat oven to 350 degrees

2 cups chopped onions
1 (4 ounce) can chopped green chiles
1 tablespoon vegetable oil
1 (28 ounce) can tomatoes, chopped
½ teaspoon garlic powder
½ teaspoon oregano
½ teaspoon salt
½ cup water
3 cups cooked and shredded
**   chicken breast**
2 cups sour cream
24 (8 inch) corn tortillas,
**   cut into 1 inch strips**
2 cups shredded mozzarella cheese

In a large skillet over medium heat, sauté onions and chiles in oil until tender. Stir in tomatoes, garlic, oregano, salt and water. Simmer 30 minutes. In a 3 quart baking dish, combine chicken and sour cream. Arrange tortilla strips over chicken. Pour tomato mixture over tortillas. Top with cheese and bake 30 minute.

Makes 10 servings   Mild

Store garlic at room temperature in a ventilated container.

Easy Chicken Enchilada Casserole

Preheat oven to 375 degrees

4 chicken breasts, cooked and cubed
1 pint sour cream
1 (10³/₄ ounce) can cream of chicken soup
1 (10³/₄ ounce) can chicken broth
1 (4 ounce) can green chiles,
**   drained and chopped**
2 cups shredded Monterey Jack cheese
6 (6 inch) corn tortillas

In a large bowl combine chicken breasts, sour cream, cream of chicken, chicken broth, and green chiles. In a greased 9 X 13 pan alternate layering the chicken mixture with the corn tortillas, top with cheese. Bake for 30 minutes or until brown.

Serves 8   Mild

 A medium size clove of garlic equals ¹/₈ teaspoon of garlic powder.

Pinto Bean Casserole

Preheat oven to 350 degrees

1 pound ground beef
1 (14¹/₂ ounce) can pinto beans, drained
1 (16 ounce) jar salsa
2 (8¹/₂ ounce) packages cornbread/
**   muffin mix**

In a large skillet over medium high heat, brown meat. Drain grease. Add beans and salsa to meat. Pour into a 9 x 13 inch baking dish. Prepare cornbread according to package. Spread cornbread batter over meat mixture. Bake for 25 minutes.

Makes 8 servings   Mild

Taco Casserole

Preheat oven to 325 degrees

1 pound lean ground beef
1 onion, chopped
1 (1.25 ounce) package taco seasoning
1 (15 1/2 ounce) can kidney beans,
   drained and rinsed
4 (10 inch) flour tortillas
2 cups shredded cheddar cheese
1 tomato, chopped
1 (4 ounce) can sliced black olives, drained
1 cup salsa

In a large skillet over medium high heat, brown ground beef and onion. Drain grease. Add taco seasoning and prepare according to package. Add kidney beans to skillet and cook for 5 minutes. In a greased 9 x 13 inch baking pan arrange flour tortillas in bottom. Spoon beef mixture over top of tortillas. Sprinkle cheese over beef mixture. Place tomatoes, black olives, and salsa over cheese. Bake for 15 minutes or until the cheese is melted.

Makes 8 servings   Mild

Do not add cold water to beans while cooking. It will cause the beans to break open.

Chicken Taco Casserole

Preheat oven to 350 degrees

1 pound chicken, cooked and shredded
1 (10 3/4 ounce) can condensed cream
of chicken soup
1 (14 1/2 ounce) can diced tomatoes
1 (4 ounce) can green chiles, diced
1 (1 1/2 ounce) package taco seasoning
4 cups crushed tortilla chips, divided
1 cup shredded cheddar cheese
2 cups shredded lettuce
1 1/2 cups sour cream
1/2 cup sliced black olives
1/4 cup chopped onions

In a 2 quart baking dish, combine
chicken, soup, tomatoes, chiles, taco
seasoning, and 2 cups tortilla chips, mix
well. Top with cheddar cheese. Bake 20
minutes. Garnish with lettuce, sour cream,
onions, black olives, and remaining
tortilla chips.

Makes 6 servings   Mild

To keep
cheese
from
sticking together
when freezing
grated cheese,
add a teaspoon
of baking soda
and shake well.

Bean Burrito Casserole

Preheat oven to 350 degrees

1 (16 ounce) can refried beans
1 (8 ounce) jar salsa
1 (4 ounce) can chopped green chiles,
   drained
1 teaspoon chili powder
1 teaspoon onion powder
1 teaspoon garlic powder
1 teaspoon ground cumin
4 (8 inch) flour tortillas
2 cups shredded cheddar cheese

In a medium bowl, combine all ingredients except flour tortillas and cheese. In a greased 9 inch pie pan, place a tortilla. Spread 1/4 of bean mixture over top, sprinkle with 1/2 cup of shredded cheese. Repeat process three more times. Bake for 35 minutes.

Makes 6 servings   Medium

Clean and disinfect your wood cutting board by rubbing it with baking soda then spray on white vinegar. Let stand for 5 minutes, rinse.

Black Bean and Rice Casserole

Preheat oven to 350 degrees

1 (15 ounce) can black beans, drained and rinsed
1 (10 ounce) can tomatoes and green chiles, chopped
1 (8 ounce) can tomato sauce
1 (8 ounce) jar salsa
2 cups rice, cooked
1 cup sour cream
2 cups shredded cheddar cheese, divided

In a large bowl, combine beans, tomatoes and chiles, tomato sauce, and salsa. Add rice, sour cream, and 1 cup of cheddar cheese, mix well. Pour mixture into a 13 x 9 x 2 inch baking dish. Sprinkle remaining cheese over bean mixture. Bake uncovered for 29 minutes or until cheese is fully melted.

Makes 6 servings   Mild

Cut grease on your dishes by adding 1 tablespoon of vinegar to hot soapy water.

Chicken Tamale Casserole

Preheat oven to 400 degrees

**1 (8 1/2 ounce) package cornbread/
  muffin mix**
1 egg
1/3 cup milk
1/2 cup shredded cheddar cheese
2 cups cooked and shredded chicken
**1 (10 3/4 ounce) can condensed cream
  of chicken soup**
1 cup corn
1/2 cup chopped green onions
1 teaspoon garlic salt
3/4 teaspoon chili powder

In a medium bowl, combine cornbread
mix, egg, milk, and cheese. In a lightly greased
9 inch pie pan, spread cornbread mixture on
bottom and up sides of pan. In a large saucepan
combine chicken, soup, corn, onions, garlic salt,
and chili powder, heat through. Pour chicken
mixture over cornbread mixture. Bake
25 minutes.

Makes 4 servings   Mild

Parsley
and
cilantro
can be frozen.
Wash and pat
dry, chop
and put in a
freezer bag.

Hot Tamales

Preheat oven to 350 degrees

8 frozen tamales
2 cups cooked and shredded chicken
4 green onions, chopped with tops
1 1/2 cups shredded cheddar cheese

Prepare tamales according to package.
Place tamales in a 9 x 9 inch baking dish.
Layer chicken, onions, and cheese. Bake
for 10 minutes or until cheese is melted.

Makes 4 servings   Mild

Nacho Tator Tot Casserole

Preheat oven to 350 degrees

2 pounds ground beef
1 cup chopped onions
2 green bell peppers, chopped
2 (10 3/4 ounce) cans condensed nacho
  cheese soup
2 (10 3/4 ounce) condensed cream of
  mushroom soup
1 bag frozen tator tots

In a large skillet over medium high heat, brown hamburger, onion, and peppers. Drain grease. Stir in soup, mix well. Pour hamburger mixture into a 13 x 9 inch baking dish. Top with tator tots. Bake for 45 minutes or until tator tots are golden brown.

Makes 8 servings   Mild

Nacho Casserole

Preheat oven to 350 degrees

1 (16 ounce) bag frozen hashbrowns
2 (10 3/4 ounce) cans condensed nacho
  cheese soup
1 (14 1/2 ounce) can diced tomatoes
  and green chiles

In a large bowl, combine all ingredients, mix well. Pour into a lightly greased 9 x 13 inch baking dish. Bake for 30 minutes.

Makes 10 servings   Medium

Mayonnaise: Was first called mahonnaise. Its present name came from a printing error in an early cookbook.

Chaco Canyon Casserole

Preheat oven to 350 degrees

1 pound ground beef
1/2 cup chopped onions
1 clove garlic, minced
1 (10 3/4 ounce) can condensed cream
  of mushroom soup
1 (11 ounce) can Mexican style corn, drained
2 (4 ounce) cans green chiles, diced
1 (12 ounce) package tortilla chips, crushed
1 (10 ounce) can enchilada sauce
2 cups shredded cheddar cheese

In a large skillet over medium high heat, brown beef with onion and garlic. Drain grease. Add soup, corn, and green chiles, mix well. Layer meat mixture, tortilla chips, and enchilada sauce in a 3 quart baking dish. Top with cheese. Bake for 30 minutes.

Makes 6 servings   Medium

Olive oil is not a good choice for deep frying because of its low smoking point.

Tortilla Chicken Casserole

Preheat oven to 350 degrees

2 cups crushed tortilla chips
2 cups cooked and cubed chicken
1 (16 ounce) can cream style corn
3/4 cup salsa
1/2 cup sliced black olives
2 green onions, chopped with tops
1 cup shredded cheddar cheese

In a 2 quart baking dish, layer ingredients in order. Bake for 40 minutes.

Makes 4 servings   Mild

Queso Loco Casserole

Preheat oven to 375 degrees

1 pound extra lean ground beef
1 (1.5 ounce) package taco seasoning
3 cups Bisquick®
3/4 cup water
1¼ cups condensed nacho cheese soup
1 green pepper, chopped
2 tablespoons onion, chopped
1½ cups thick and chunky salsa
1½ cups cheddar cheese, shredded
½ cup sour cream

In a large skillet over medium high heat, brown ground beef. Drain grease. Add taco seasoning and prepare according to directions on package. In a small bowl, mix Bisquick® and water. Spread dough evenly in a greased 9 x 13 x 2 inch baking pan. Spoon ground beef evenly over dough. Spread evenly, nacho cheese soup over beef. Sprinkle green pepper and onion over soup. Spread thick and chunky salsa over pepper and onions. Top with cheddar cheese. Bake for 35 minutes. Garnish with dollops of sour cream.

Makes 8 servings   Medium

 Red peppers have more vitamin A then green or yellow peppers.

Chili Bake

Preheat oven to 350 degrees

1 (15 1/2 ounce) can no bean chili
1 (7 ounce) can diced green chile peppers
3 tablespoons chopped onion
1 cup shredded cheddar cheese

Pour chili into a 9 x 9 inch baking dish.
Top with green chiles, onion and cheese.
Bakes for 20 minutes

Makes 4 servings   Medium

Taco in Spanish means a sandwich made with a tortilla.

Salsa Chicken Bake

Preheat oven to 375 degrees

1 (12 ounce) jar salsa
2 cups shredded Velveeta® cheese
3 cups cooked and shredded chicken
4 (8 inch) flour tortillas

In a medium saucepan over medium heat,
combine salsa and cheese. Cook until cheese is
melted. Reserve 1 1/2 cup of salsa mixture. Stir
chicken into remaining salsa mixture. Spoon
chicken mixture down the center of each
tortilla. Roll tortillas and place seam side down
in a 9 x 9 inch baking dish. Pour remaining
salsa over tortillas. Cover and bake for
20 minutes.

Makes 4 servings   Mild

Tex-Mex Casserole

Preheat oven to 350 degree

1 (10³/₄ ounce) can condensed cream
  of chicken soup
1 (10³/₄ ounce) can condensed cream
  of mushroom soup
1 (14¹/₂ ounce) can diced tomatoes
  and green chile peppers
1 cup canned chicken broth
2 (8 ounce) cans chili beans, drained
1 cup chopped onion
¹/₂ cup diced red bell pepper
12 (8 inch) flour tortillas, quartered
4 chicken breasts, cooked and diced
3 cups shredded Mexican style cheese

In a large saucepan over medium heat,
combine soups, tomatoes and chiles,
chicken broth, beans, onion, bell pepper.
Heat through. In a 13 x 9 inch casserole dish,
layer 4 tortillas, ¹/₂ of diced chicken, ¹/₃ of
soup mixture 4 more tortillas, remaining
chicken ¹/₃ more of the soup, 4 more
tortillas, and remaining soup mixture.
Top with cheese. Bake for 25 minutes.

Makes 8 servings   Mild

To slice tomatoes use a serrated knife. Hold tomato so the stem faces out. Slice off end and discard; continue to slice in quick cuts.

Polo Pot Pie

Preheat oven to 400 degrees

1 (10 3/4 ounce) can condensed cream
   of chicken soup
1/2 cup sour cream
1/2 cup salsa
2 teaspoons chili powder
4 green onions, chopped with tops
3 cups cooked and cubed chicken
1 (11 1/2 ounce) package refrigerated
   cornbread twists

In a 2 quart baking dish, combine all ingredients except the corn bread twists. Bake covered for 15 minutes. Remove from oven and stir. Separate cornbread twists into individual strips. Weave strips across the top of the baking dish. Secure edge of twists over the side of baking dish. Bake an additional 15 minutes or until cornbread twists are golden.

Makes 6 servings   Mild

Tabasco: Some historians say it's a Central American Indian word that means "land where the soil is hot and humid".

A-Maize-ing Casserole

Preheat oven to 375 degrees

2 (8 1/2 ounce) packages corn bread/muffin mix
1 (14 3/4 ounce) can cream style corn
1 (15 1/4 ounce) can whole kernel corn, drained
1 (4 ounce) can diced green chiles
1 cup shredded Monterey Jack cheese

Prepare corn bread according to package directions. In a lightly greased 9 x 13 inch baking dish pour half of batter. In a medium bowl combine corns. Pour over batter. Top with chiles and cheese. Spread remaining corn bread batter on top. Bake 30 minutes.

Makes 10 servings   Mild

Fire Hose Casserole

Preheat oven to 350 degrees

4 chicken breasts, boneless,
   cooked and cubed
1/2 cup diced green pepper
1/4 cup diced onion
1 (10 3/4 ounce) can condensed nacho
   cheese soup
1 (14 1/2 ounce) can diced tomatoes
   and green chiles
1 (4 ounce) can sliced black olives,
   drained
8 ounces processed cheese, cut in cubes
6 ounce mushrooms, sliced and divided
1 (8 ounce) package thin spaghetti,
   cooked and drained

In a large bowl, combine chicken, pepper, onion, soup, tomatoes and chiles, black olives, cheese, 3 ounces mushroom. Add spaghetti, mix well. Pour spaghetti mixture into a lightly greased 9 x 13 inch baking pan. Top with remaining mushrooms. Bake for 25 minutes.

Makes 8 servings   Mild

 Tabasco was first sold commercially in 1868. A two ounce bottle of Tabasco contains at least 720 drops.

Towering Tortilla Casserole

Preheat oven to 350 degrees

1 (16 ounce) can refried beans
1 (8 ounce) can tomato sauce
1 (4 ounce) can chopped green chiles
1 teaspoon chili powder
1 teaspoon ground cumin
1 teaspoon garlic powder
1 teaspoon onion powder
4 (8 inch) flour tortillas
2 cups shredded cheddar cheese

To remove food stains from your hands, pour lemon juice on hands and rub, then rinse.

In a medium bowl, combine beans, tomato sauce, green chiles, chili powder, cumin, garlic powder, and onion powder. Mix well. In a lightly greased 8 x 8 inch bake pan, place 1 tortilla. Spread ¼ cup of bean mixture over tortilla. Layer another tortilla and an additional ¼ cup bean mixture. Sprinkle 1 cup of cheese over tortilla. Layer tortilla over cheese, spread ¼ cup of bean mixture over tortilla. Top with remaining tortilla, spread with remaining bean mixture. Top with cheese. Bake for 35 minutes.

Makes 4 servings   Medium

Casa Casserole

Preheat oven to 400 degrees

1 (24 ounce) package frozen hash
   browns
2 tablespoons butter or margarine
1/4 pound hot link sausage, cooked
   and crumbled
2 cups shredded pepper jack cheese
6 eggs, beaten
1 (4 ounce) can diced green chiles
2 tomatoes, sliced
1/4 cup shredded Parmesan cheese

In a large skillet over medium high heat,
brown hash browns in butter. In a large bowl,
combine hash browns, sausage, cheese, eggs,
chiles, mix well. Pour into a lightly greased
9 x 13 inch baking dish. Bake for 25 minutes.
Arrange tomatoes on top. Sprinkle with
Parmesan cheese. Broil for 2 minutes.

Makes 6 servings   Medium

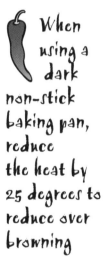

When using a dark non-stick baking pan, reduce the heat by 25 degrees to reduce over browning

Vega Veggie Casserole

Preheat oven to 375 degrees

1 (8 ounce) package refrigerated crescent rolls
1 (8 ounce) package cream cheese, softened
2 tablespoons mayonnaise
1 tablespoon salsa
1/2 cup chopped green bell pepper
1/2 cup chopped onion
1/2 cup peeled and chopped carrot
1/2 cup chopped mushrooms
1 1/2 cups shredded cheddar cheese

Pat crescent rolls into bottom of an ungreased 13 x 9 inch baking dish. Bake for 8 minutes or until golden brown. Set aside to cool. In a small bowl, combine cream cheese, mayonnaise, and salsa, mix well. Spread cheese mixture over crust. In a medium bowl, combine pepper, onion, carrot, and mushrooms. Layer over cream cheese. Top with cheddar cheese. Broil 5 minutes or until cheese is melted. Cut and serve warm.

Makes 12 servings   Mild

An 8 ounce package of cream cheese is equivalent to 1 cup.

Rio Grande Quiche

Preheat oven to 375 degrees

1 pound pork sausage, browned
1 cup shredded Monterey Jack cheese
1 cup shredded cheddar cheese
1/2 cup minced onion
1 (4 ounce) can diced green chiles
1 jalapeno pepper, minced
10 eggs, beaten
1 teaspoon chili powder
1 teaspoon ground cumin
1 teaspoon salt
1/2 teaspoon pepper
1/2 teaspoon garlic powder

In a 13 x 9 inch baking dish, layer sausage, cheese, onion, green chiles, and Jalapeno. In a medium bowl, mix eggs and seasonings. Pour egg mixture into baking dish. Bake for 25 minutes.

Makes 8 servings   Wild & Hot

Chile Quiche

Preheat oven to 350 degrees

1 (4 ounce) can diced green chiles
2 cups shredded mozzarella cheese
2 green onions, chopped with tops
1 (4 ounce) carton egg beaters

Place chiles in a lightly greased 9 x 9 inch baking dish. Sprinkle cheese and onion over chiles. Pour egg beaters over mixture in baking dish. Bake 20 minutes.

Makes 6 servings   Mild

To test if an egg is fresh, place it in a bowl of salty water. If it sinks it is fresh, if it floats it is old and should be discarded.

Beef + Bean Burrito Casserole

Preheat oven to 350 degrees

1 pound ground beef
1 (15¹/₂ ounce) can refried beans
1 (10 inch) package flour tortillas
1 (11 ounce) can enchilada sauce
2 tablespoons diced green chiles
**1 (16 ounce) package shredded
   cheddar cheese**

In a large skillet over medium high heat, brown ground beef. Drain grease. Add refried beans, mix well. Place bean mixture in the middle of each tortilla, roll and place in 9 x13 inch baking dish. Pour enchilada sauce evenly over tortillas. Sprinkle green chiles then cheese over sauce. Bake 30 minutes.

Makes 6 servings   Medium

Choose Plum tomatoes when making sauce or when making thick and chunky salsa. They have fewer seeds and contain less water.

Wild Oats

Breads & Rolls

Everyone's Favorite Taco Shells

4 cups flour
2 tablespoons oil
¼ teaspoon salt
2 teaspoons baking powder
1¼ cups cold water

Combine all ingredients in a medium bowl with a pastry blender and then use hands until dough reaches a rollable consistency. Break off 1½ to 2 inch piece of dough, make a ball. Roll on floured surface until very thin, make a 4 to 6 inch circle. Fill with taco meat, fold in half and crimp edges. Fry in vegetable oil at 375 degrees until golden brown. Remove and drain on paper towel. Unfold edges and top with your favorite taco toppings.

Makes 20, 5 inch shells

Flour Tortillas

3 cups flour
1 teaspoon salt
⅓ cup vegetable shortening
1 cup warm water

In a large bowl, using a pastry blender, combine flour, salt, and shortening until crumbly. Add water and mix until dough forms a ball. On a lightly floured surface knead dough for 5 minutes. Cover and let stand for 30 minutes. Divide dough into 12 equal parts and roll into a ball shape. On a lightly floured surface, roll each ball into an 8 inch circle. Layer tortillas between wax paper. In a large heavy skillet, over high heat, place tortilla and cook on each side for 30 seconds.

Makes 12 tortillas

Tortillas called the bread of Mexico, were originally used as a plate or spoon.

Corn Tortillas

2 cups instant corn flour
1¹/₃ cups warm water

In a medium size bowl, combine corn flour and water. If dough is too crumbly it needs more water, if it is sticky it needs more flour. Pinch off enough dough to make a 2 inch ball. On a lightly floured surface roll the dough into a thin circle. In a non-stick skillet, on high heat, cook tortilla on each side for 1 minute, turning only once.

Makes 8 tortillas

 You can freeze tortillas for up to 6 months.

Wheat Tortillas

¹/₂ cup vegetable shortening
4 cups wheat flour
1 teaspoon salt
1 cup water

In a medium bowl, cut shortening into flour. Dissolve salt in water. Add water slowly, mixing it into flour and shortening. On a lightly floured surface, knead dough for 5 minutes. It should be smooth and elastic. Divide into 10 equal ball shapes of dough. Cover and let stand in a warm place for 15 minutes. Flatten balls and roll out to 6 inches in diameter. Stretch tortillas gently to make very thin. In a skillet on high heat, cook tortilla for a few seconds on each side.

Makes 10 tortillas

Indian Fry Bread

3 cups flour
1¹/₄ teaspoons baking powder
1 teaspoon salt
1¹/₃ cups warm water
³/₄ cup shortening

In a medium bowl, combine flour, baking powder and salt. Mix in water. Knead until dough is soft. Roll out to thin 5 inch pancakes. Fry in shortening until golden brown.

Makes 8

Mexican Cornbread

Preheat oven to 400 degrees

1 (8¹/₂ ounce) package self-rising cornmeal
1 egg
¹/₂ cup milk
1 (8 ounce) can cream style corn
1 cup shredded Monterey Jack Cheese
1 (4 ounce) can diced green chile peppers, drained

Place cornmeal in a large bowl. Stir in egg, milk, creamed corn, cheese, and chiles. Spread batter in a lightly greased 8 x 8 inch baking pan. Bake for 25 minutes or until golden brown and cornbread pulls away from sides of pan.

Makes 12 servings

 To test if an egg is hard boiled or fresh, place on the counter and spin. If it wobbles as it spins it is fresh. If it spins smoothly it is hard boiled.

Low Fat Mexican Cornbread

Preheat oven to 400 degrees

1 teaspoon butter or margarine
1 cup chopped red bell pepper
1 cup whole kernel corn
1^{1}/$_{3}$ cups self rising cornmeal
^{2}/$_{3}$ cup self-rising flour
1 teaspoon sugar
^{1}/$_{8}$ teaspoon ground red pepper
1^{1}/$_{4}$ cups fat free milk
2 egg whites, lightly beaten

In a large skillet, over medium high, melt butter. Lightly brown red bell pepper and corn. Cool corn mixture. In a large bowl, combine corn meal, flour, sugar, and ground red pepper. Add corn mixture, mix well. Add milk and egg whites, stir until moist. Coat a 9-inch round cake pan with vegetable oil. Pour batter into pan and bake for 30 minutes.

Makes 8 servings

Place aluminum foil under the napkin in your breadbasket to keep bread warm longer.

Sour Cream Cornbread

Preheat oven to 400 degrees

1 cup sour cream
1 cup self-rising cornmeal
3 eggs
1 cup cream style corn

In a large bowl, combine all ingredients, mix well. Pour into a greased 8 x 8 baking pan. Bake for 30 to 40 minutes.

Makes 4 to 6 servings

Sausage Cornbread

Preheat oven to 375 degrees

1 pound ground sausage
1 small onion, chopped
1¹/₂ cups self-rising cornmeal
2 eggs
¹/₄ cup chopped green pepper
1 (8 ounce) can cream style corn
1¹/₂ cups shredded cheddar cheese

In a large skillet, brown sausage and onion over medium high heat. Drain grease and set aside. In a large bowl, combine cornmeal, eggs, green pepper, creamed corn, mix well. Pour half of batter into a lightly greased 9 x 13 inch pan. Sprinkle sausage mixture and cheese over batter. Pour remaining batter over top. Bake for 40 minutes.

Makes 12 servings

Canyon Cornbread

Preheat oven to 400 degrees

2 eggs
¹/₂ cup Miracle Whip®
¹/₄ teaspoon ground red pepper
1 (8.75 ounce) can corn, drained
1 (8.5 ounce) package corn muffin mix
¹/₂ cup chopped onion
¹/₃ cup diced red bell pepper
1 (4 ounce) can chopped green chiles

In a medium bowl, combine eggs, Miracle Whip®, red pepper. Add remaining ingredients, stir till just mixed. Pour into a greased 8 x 8 inch baking pan. Bake for 25 minutes

Makes 6 servings

Quick Clean Up: Remove cooked on food in your non-stick skillet by filling it with water, heat until boiling, pour out water, wipe away loose food.

Jalapeno Bread

Preheat oven to 350 degrees

1¹/₂ teaspoons dry active yeast
¹/₂ cup warm water
1¹/₃ cups bread flour
¹/₂ cup cornmeal
1 teaspoon salt
1 tablespoon sugar
1 tablespoon butter
³/₄ cup whole kernel corn
1 tablespoon chopped and seeded
** Jalapeno pepper**

In a small bowl, combine yeast and warm water, mix and set aside. In a large bowl, combine flour, cornmeal, salt, and sugar. Using a pastry cutter, cut butter into flour mixture. Add yeast mixture, mix well. Add corn and Jalapeno pepper, mix well. On a lightly flour surface, knead until smooth. Return dough to large bowl and cover with a dishtowel. Let rise in a warm place for 90 minutes. Place in a large greased loaf pan. Brush a small amount of butter on top of bread, let rise for an additional 30 minutes. Bake for 35 minutes or until bread is golden brown.

Makes 1 loaf

To help bread dough rise, heat a damp towel in the dryer then wrap around base of the bowl that the bread is in.

Pan de Muerto: Bread of the Dead

Preheat oven to 350 degrees

¹/₄ cup sugar
¹/₄ cup milk
¹/₄ cup butter
¹/₂ teaspoon salt
¹/₄ cup warm water
1 package active dry yeast
2 eggs
3 cups flour, unsifted
2 teaspoons sugar
¹/₂ teaspoon anise seed
¹/₄ teaspoon cinnamon

In a small saucepan bring to a boil ¹/₄ cup sugar, milk, butter, and salt. In a large bowl, mix warm water and dry yeast until dissolved, let stand 5 minutes. Add milk to mixture. In a small bowl, separate yolk from egg whites, reserve egg whites for later use. Add yolk to yeast mixture, mix well. Add flour to yeast mixture, mix until a ball forms. On a lightly floured surface, knead dough until smooth. Return to large bowl and cover with a dishtowel. Let rise in a warm place for 90 minutes. Knead dough again on a floured surface. Divide dough into fourths, setting one fourth aside. Roll the three sections into ropes. On a greased baking sheet, pinch rope ends together and braid. Pinch other end together when finish braiding. Divide remaining dough in half and form two bones. Cross and lay atop braided loaf. Cover bread with a towel and let rise for 30 minutes. In a small bowl, combine 2 teaspoons sugar, anise seed, and cinnamon. Beat lightly, the egg whites that were reserved. When 30 minutes are up, brush top of bread with egg white and sprinkle sugar mixture on top, except on top of cross bones. Bake for 35 minutes.

Makes 10 servings

Bread of the Dead is served during the Day of the Dead celebration. Rather than being a morbid occasion, it is a festive time.

211

Spanish Bread

Preheat oven to 450 degrees

3 cups warm water
1¹/₂ tablespoons dry active yeast
7 cups flour
2 teaspoons salt
¹/₄ cup olive oil

In a medium size bowl combine water and yeast. In a large bowl, mix flour and salt, run through a sifter into the large bowl. Using your hands, mix in olive oil. Slowly pour yeast mixture into flour, work to form a firm dough. On a lightly floured surface, knead dough until it becomes elastic. Grease the large bowl and place dough back in it. Cover with a damp towel, and set in a warm place until it has doubled in size, approximately 45 minutes. Remove dough and knead once again, until smooth. Return to bowl and let rise 10 minutes. Divide dough into two parts and place in greased loaf pans. Cut a slit down the center of each loaf. Let bread rise for 30 minutes, or until the tops begins to flatten. Bake for 45 minutes or until bread is golden brown and make a hollow sound when you knock on top of bread. Remove bread from pans and let cool.

Makes 2 loaves

Freeze yeast to extend its shelf life.

Taco Bread

Preheat oven to 375 degrees

2/3 cup warm water
1 1/2 teaspoons active dry yeast
3 1/3 cups flour
4 1/2 teaspoons sugar
3 tablespoons taco seasoning
1 1/2 teaspoons dried parsley flakes
1 teaspoon salt
1/2 cup sour cream
3 tablespoons salsa

In a small bowl combine water and yeast, mix well and set aside. In a large bowl, combine flour, sugar, taco seasoning, parsley flakes, and salt, mix well. In a small bowl combine sour cream and salsa. Make a well in the center of flour mixture, stir in sour cream and salsa, and yeast mixture. Using hands mix ingredients until dough forms a ball. On a lightly floured surface, knead dough until elastic. Grease bowl and return dough, cover and place in a warm place for 45 minutes. Knead dough for 5 minutes then place in a greased loaf pan. Cover and let rise for 30 minutes. Bake for 30 minutes.

Makes 1 loaf

 If you do not have a rolling pin, fill a jar with cold water and use as you would a rolling pin.

Clovis Cheese Bread

Preheat oven to 350 degrees

1¹/₂ cups milk
1 egg
3 ³/₄ cups Bisquick®
³/₄ cup shredded cheddar cheese

In a small bowl, combine milk, egg, and Bisquick® mix. Fold in cheese. Pour into a lightly greased loaf pan. Bake 1 hour or until golden brown.

Makes 1 loaf

Plastic wrap will stick to the edge of your bowl if you wet the edges of the bowl first.

Pepper Bread

1 green pepper, diced
1 red pepper, diced
1 yellow pepper, diced
1 cup sliced onion
3 garlic cloves, minced
5 tablespoons vegetable oil, divided
¹/₂ teaspoon garlic salt
¹/₂ teaspoon dried basil
1 loaf French bread
1 cup shredded mozzarella cheese

In a large skillet, sauté peppers, onion, and garlic cloves in 2 tablespoons oil until tender. Add garlic salt and basil, set aside. Cut bread into 1 inch slices. Place on an ungreased baking sheet. Broil each side for 1 to 2 minutes or until lightly browned. Brush remaining oil on one side of bread. Top with pepper mixture and cheese. Broil for 2 to 3 minutes or until cheese is melted.

Makes 1 dozen

Cheese Bites Bread

Preheat oven to 400 degrees

1 (3 ounce) package cream cheese
1/2 cup butter or margarine
1/4 pound cheddar cheese, shredded
2 egg whites, stiffly beaten
1 loaf French bread,
   sliced into 1 inch cubes

In a medium size saucepan, melt cream cheese, butter, and cheddar cheese till smooth. Remove from heat; fold in egg whites. Dip bread cubes in cheese mixture until well coated, place on an ungreased cookie sheet. Bake for 15 minutes or until brown.

Makes 4 dozen

Zorro's Zucchini Bread

Preheat oven to 350 degrees

6 cups flour
4 cups grated zucchini
1 cup chocolate chips
2 teaspoons cinnamon
2 teaspoons baking powder
2 teaspoons salt
6 eggs
4 cups sugar
2 cups vegetable oil
2 teaspoons vanilla

In a large bowl combine, flour, zucchini, chocolate chips, cinnamon, baking powder, and salt. In a small bowl combine, eggs, sugar, vegetable oil, and vanilla, mix well. Add egg mixture to dry ingredients, mix well. Lightly grease 3 loaf pans, pour batter in. Bake for 1 hour and 15 minutes.

Makes 3 loafs

Quick Clean Up: Spray your cheese grater with non-stick spray before use.

De Plano Bread

2 cups flour
1/4 teaspoon salt
2/3 cup water
1/4 cup sugar
vegetable oil

In a medium bowl, combine flour, salt and water; mix well. On a lightly floured surface, knead dough for 3 minutes. Divide into 12 evenly sized balls. Roll each ball into a round flat shape. Sprinkle sugar on top of each round bread. Fold in quarters and roll out again. In a large skillet heat 1 inch of vegetable oil. Fry on each side until golden brown. Drain on paper towel.

Makes 12 flat breads

To store homemade breads for more than a few days, wrap in aluminum foil or plastic wrap.

Cilantro Bread

Preheat oven to 350 degrees

1/2 cup butter, melted
1 egg
1 tablespoon minced cilantro
1 teaspoon garlic salt
1 (1 pound) loaf frozen bread dough,
  thawed

In a small bowl combine, butter, egg, cilantro, and garlic salt. Pull off golf ball size pieces of dough; dip in butter mixture and place in a greased bunt pan. Pour remaining butter mixture over dough. Place in a warm place until dough has doubled. Bake for 35 minutes or until golden brown.

Makes 1 loaf

Spanish Spoon Bread

Preheat oven to 350 degrees

¹/₂ cup butter, softened
¹/₃ cup masa harina
¹/₄ cup water
1¹/₂ cups whole kernel corn
¹/₃ cup sugar
¹/₄ cup cornmeal
¹/₂ teaspoon baking powder
¹/₄ teaspoon salt
2 tablespoons heavy whipping cream

In a medium bowl, using a mixer beat butter until creamy. Mix in masa harina and water, mix well. In a blender process corn till slightly chunky; pour into butter mixture. In a small bowl combine sugar, cornmeal, baking powder, salt, and heavy whipping cream; pour into butter mixture, mix well. Pour batter into an ungreased 8 x 8 inch baking pan, cover with foil. Place pan in a 9 x 13 inch baking pan, fill pan to ¹/₃ of the way up with water. Bake for 1 hour. Remove and cool for 10 minutes.

Makes 6 servings

 To lower the cholesterol in a recipe calling for eggs, substitute 2 egg whites for a whole egg.

Cimarron Cinnamon Bread

Preheat oven to 350 degrees

2 cups flour
1 cup sugar
1 cup buttermilk
$^1/_4$ cup vegetable oil
2 eggs
2 teaspoons baking powder
2 teaspoons vanilla
$1^1/_2$ teaspoons cinnamon
1 teaspoon salt
$^1/_2$ teaspoon baking soda
2 tablespoons sugar
1 teaspoon cinnamon
2 tablespoons butter

In a large bowl, combine flour, 1 cup sugar, buttermilk, vegetable oil, eggs, baking powder, vanilla, $1^1/_2$ teaspoon cinnamon, salt, and baking soda, mix well. Pour batter into a greased 9 x 5 inch loaf pan. In a small bowl, combine 2 tablespoons sugar and 1 teaspoon cinnamon. Cut in butter till crumbly. Sprinkle over top of batter. Using a butter knife, swirl top of bread to get a marbled look. Bake 50 minutes.

Makes 1 loaf

Test loaves of bread by tapping the top with your finger. A hollow sound means the loaf is perfectly baked.

Olé Onion Bread

Preheat oven to 375 degrees

1/2 cup chopped onion
1 tablespoon butter or margarine
1 1/2 cups baking mix
1/2 cup milk
1 egg, beaten
1 cup shredded cheddar cheese, divided
2 tablespoons chopped parsley
2 tablespoons butter or margarine

In a skillet over medium heat, sauté onion in butter until tender. In a medium bowl, combine baking mix, milk, egg, 1/2 cup cheddar cheese, parsley, and sautéed onion. Stir until just moistened. Pour batter into a lightly greased 8 x 8 inch baking pan. Dot the 2 tablespoons of butter on top of batter, sprinkle 1/2 cup cheddar cheese on mixture, bake 20 minutes or until edges are brown.

Makes 8 servings

Yeast is a living organism with 3200 billion cells to the pound and no two are alike.

Pronto Rolls

Preheat oven to 350 degrees

1 (8 ounce) brown and serve rolls
2 tablespoons butter or margarine
1/4 teaspoon garlic salt
1 teaspoon minced cilantro

Place rolls on a baking sheet. Brush with butter. Sprinkle with garlic salt and cilantro. Bake for 35 minutes or until golden brown.

Makes 6 servings

Torta Rolls

Preheat oven to 350 degrees

2¹/₂ cups warm water
1 ounce dry active yeast
8¹/₂ cups flour
2 teaspoons sugar
2 teaspoons salt

In a medium size bowl, dissolve yeast in water. In a large bowl, combine flour, sugar, and salt. Make a well in the center of flour mixture, pour in dissolved yeast, mix well. Cover with a damp cloth and place in a warm place for 90 minutes. On a lightly floured surface knead dough until smooth. Roll into 20 equal sized balls. Brush each roll with vegetable oil and dust with flour. Flatten with your hand into an oblong shape. Place on a baking sheet. Using a dull knife, score the top of each roll with two lines. Cover rolls and set in a warm place for 30 minutes. Bake for 30 minutes or until golden brown.

Makes 20

Cinnamon comes from the inner skin of the cassia tree bark.

Gonzales Glazed Rolls

Preheat oven to 350 degrees

24 frozen dinner rolls
1 (3 ounce) package butterscotch pudding
1 teaspoon cinnamon
¹/₂ cup brown sugar
¹/₂ cup butter

Place rolls in a well greased cake pan. Sprinkle butterscotch pudding and cinnamon on top of each roll. In a small saucepan, bring brown sugar and butter to a boil, pour over rolls. Cover and let rise over night. Bake for 30 minutes or until golden brown.

Makes 24 rolls

Cochineria Rolls

Preheat oven to 325

1 (18-24) package frozen rolls
1 (4 ounce) box butterscotch pudding
4 tablespoons butter or margarine
1/2 cup brown sugar

While rolls are still frozen, cut in half. Arrange around the bottom of a lightly greased bunt pan. Sprinkle dry pudding over rolls. In a small saucepan heat butter and brown sugar. Pour over pudding and rolls. Let rise in a warm place until dough has doubled in size. Bake for 35 minutes.

Makes 1 loaf

Tabasco Biscuits

Preheat oven to 375 degrees.

2 cups flour
1 tablespoon baking powder
1/2 teaspoon salt
1/3 cup vegetable shortening
1/3 cup chopped green onion
2 dashes Tabasco®
3/4 cup milk

In a large bowl, combine flour, baking powder, and salt. Cut in shortening into flour mixture until mixture is crumbly. Stir in onion. In a small bowl combine Tabasco and milk. Make a well in the middle of flour mixture. Pour milk into well; stir until dough comes together. On a lightly floured surface, knead dough for 1 minute. On a lightly greased baking sheet, pat dough to a 1 inch thickness. Bake for 30 minutes or until lightly brown. Cut into squares.

Makes 8 squares

Baking powder loses its leavening power with age. To test and see if it is still fresh, put 1/2 teaspoon baking powder into 1/4 cup hot water. If the water bubbles a lot, the baking powder is fresh.

Mission Mustard Drop Biscuits

Preheat oven to 375 degrees

1¹/₃ cups flour
¹/₂ cup cornmeal
1¹/₂ teaspoons baking powder
¹/₂ teaspoon ground mustard
¹/₂ teaspoon salt
¹/₂ cup shortening
¹/₂ cup shredded cheddar cheese
1 cup milk

In a medium bowl, combine flour, cornmeal, baking powder ground mustard, and salt. Cut in shortening until small crumbles appear. Stir in cheese and milk, mix well. On a greased baking sheet, drop by ¹/₄ cupfuls 2 inches apart. Bake for 25 to 28 minutes or until golden brown.

Makes 10 biscuits

Refresh biscuits by putting them in a wet paper bag, seal the end of bag, bake at 300 degrees for 5 minutes.

Salsa Biscuits

Preheat oven to 450 degrees

¹/₄ cup salsa
¹/₄ cup milk
1 teaspoon Worcestershire
¹/₂ teaspoon minced onion
2 cups biscuit mix

In a large bowl, combine all ingredients except biscuit mix, let stand for 5 minutes. Add in biscuit mix; stir until a soft dough is formed. On a lightly floured surface, knead dough for 5 minutes. Roll to ¹/₂ inch thickness, cut into 2 inch round shapes. Bake on an ungreased baking sheet for 10 minutes.

Makes 10

Texarkana Tomato Drop Biscuits

Preheat oven to 425 degrees

1/2 cup finely chopped green onions
1 tablespoon vegetable oil
3/4 cup chopped and seeded tomato
4 teaspoons parsley
2 cups flour
1 tablespoon baking powder
1 teaspoon salt
1/4 teaspoon black pepper
1/4 teaspoon Cayenne pepper
1/3 cup shortening
2/3 cup milk

In a small skillet over medium heat, sauté onions in oil until tender. Add tomato and cook 1 minute. Stir in parsley, remove from heat. In a large bowl, combine flour, baking powder, salt, pepper, and Cayenne pepper. Cut in shortening until coarse crumbs form. Stir in milk and tomato mixture until combined. Drop by heaping teaspoons onto a greased baking sheet 2 inches apart. Bake for 10 to 12 minutes or until golden brown. Serve warm.

Makes 1½ dozen

 Mariachi music consists of trumpets, guitars, drums, as well as violins and harps. Men wear black suits; their pants are decorated with silver..

Fiesta Corn Muffins

Preheat oven to 375

1/2 cup sugar
1/2 cup butter or margarine
5 eggs
1 cup buttermilk
1 (4 ounce) can chopped green
   chiles, drained
1 1/4 cups cornmeal
1 cup flour
2 teaspoons baking powder
1/2 teaspoon salt
1 cup corn
1 cup shredded Monterey Jack cheese
1 cup shredded cheddar cheese

In a medium bowl, cream sugar and butter. Add eggs one at a time, beating after each addition. Beat in buttermilk and chiles. In a small bowl combine cornmeal, flour, baking powder, and salt. Gradually add flour mixture to sugar mixture, blend well. Fold in corn and cheeses. Grease the bottoms of a muffin pan. Fill each cup 3/4 full. Bake for 20 to 25 minutes or until golden brown.

Makes 1 dozen

Do not over stir muffin batter. It will make the muffins hard and they will have pointed tops.

Maize Muffins

Preheat oven to 400 degrees

2 (8 .5 ounce) boxes corn bread mix
1 (16 ounce) tub cottage cheese
1¹/₂ cups shredded cheddar cheese
5 eggs
1 cup diced onion
1 teaspoon salt
¹/₄ teaspoon pepper
¹/₂ cup butter, melted

In a large bowl, combine all ingredients, batter should be slightly lumpy. Lightly grease the bottoms of a muffin tin. Fill each cup ³/₄ full. Bake for 15 minutes or until golden brown.

Makes 2 dozen

Hidden Treasure Muffins

Preheat oven to 400 degrees

1³/₄ cups flour
¹/₂ cup sugar
1 tablespoon baking powder
¹/₂ teaspoon salt
²/₃ cup milk
2 eggs
¹/₃ cup butter or margarine, melted
1 teaspoon grated lemon peel
¹/₂ cup strawberry jam

In a large bowl, combine flour, sugar, baking powder, and salt. In a small bowl lightly beat milk, eggs, butter, and lemon peel. Pour into dry ingredients and stir till slightly lumpy. Lightly grease bottoms of muffin tin, fill cups half full. Spoon jam into middle of batter. Spoon additional batter until cup is ³/₄ full. Bake 20 minutes or until golden brown.

Makes 1 dozen

For crunchy, sugary crust on muffins, sprinkle white or brown sugar over the batter in the muffin pans before baking..

Buenos Dias Muffins

Preheat oven to 375 degrees

2 cups Bisquick®
1 egg
2/3 cup milk
1/4 cup vegetable oil
1 cup shredded cheddar cheese
8 strips bacon, cooked and crumbled

In a medium bowl, combine Bisquick®, egg, milk, and oil until just moistened. Fold in cheddar cheese and bacon. Lightly grease the bottoms of muffin tins. Fill cups 3/4 full, bake 20 minutes or until golden brown

Makes 1 dozen

Insert a toothpick in the muffin that is closest to the center, if it comes out clean the muffins are done.

Alameda Apple Muffins

Preheat oven to 400 degrees

2 cups flour
1/2 cup sugar
4 teaspoons baking powder
3/4 teaspoon salt
3/4 teaspoon cinnamon
1/4 teaspoon nutmeg
1 cup milk
1 egg, beaten
1/3 cup vegetable oil
3/4 cup chopped apple

In a large bowl, combine flour, sugar, baking powder, salt, cinnamon, and nutmeg. Add milk, egg, and vegetable oil, stir until just moistened. Fold in chopped apple. Lightly grease bottoms of muffin cups. Fill cups 3/4 full. Bake for 25 minutes.

Makes 1 dozen

Carlsbad Carrot Muffins

Preheat oven to 375 degrees

2 cups brown sugar, firmly packed
1/2 cup salad oil
4 eggs
2 cups flour
2 teaspoons baking powder
2 teaspoons lemon juice
2 teaspoons vanilla extract
1 teaspoon salt
2 cups carrots, grated

In a large bowl, combine sugar, oil, and eggs, beat well. Blend in flour, baking powder, lemon juice, vanilla extract, and salt. Stir in carrots, mix well. Lightly grease bottom of muffin cups. Fill cups 3/4 full. Bake for 30 minutes.

Makes 2 dozen

Carrots will stay fresh longer if the tops are removed before storing.

Cuatro Cheese Fritters

1/4 pound Swiss cheese, shredded
1/4 pound mozzarella cheese, shredded
1 cup grated Parmesan cheese
1/3 cup cottage cheese
1/3 cup chopped parsley
5 eggs
1 cup flour
1/2 tablespoon Cayenne pepper
1 teaspoon salt
oil for frying

In a large bowl, combine all ingredients till just blended. In a large saucepan over medium high, heat 2 inches of oil. Drop batter by tablespoon into hot oil. Fry until golden brown. Drain on a paper towel.

Makes 15 servings

Mexican Fritters

1/3 cup sugar
1/3 cup unsalted butter,
   room temperature
2 eggs
1 teaspoon vanilla
13/4 cups flour
2 teaspoons baking powder
1/2 teaspoon salt
2 tablespoons heavy cream
1 cup sugar
2 teaspoons cinnamon
oil for frying

In a large bowl, cream 1/3 cup sugar and butter. Beat in eggs and vanilla. In a medium bowl, combine flour, baking powder and salt, add to sugar mixture. Add cream and stir until it is just combined. On a floured surface, knead dough for 1 minute. Roll dough to 1/2 inch thickness. Using a floured 21/2 inch cookie cutter, cut out rounds and place on wax paper. In a small bowl, combine sugar and flour, set aside. In a large saucepan pour oil to a 11/2 inch depth, heat over high heat. Drop rounds into oil and fry until golden brown. Drain on paper towel. While still warm sprinkle with cinnamon and sugar.

Makes 20

The word Mariachi comes from the blending of the French word for Marriage and an indian word for music. They were originally hired by the French to play at weddings.

Houston Hush Puppies

2¼ cups self-rising cornmeal
3 tablespoons self rising flour
1 egg
1 cup milk
2 tablespoons chopped, canned
  diced green chiles
oil for frying

In a medium bowl, combine corn meal and flour. Add egg, milk, and green chiles. Drop by tablespoon into hot oil, fry until golden brown. Drain on paper towel.

Makes 1½ dozen

Hacienda Hush Puppies

¾ cup cornmeal
½ cup flour
1½ teaspoons baking powder
½ teaspoon salt
¼ teaspoon ground red pepper
1 cup shredded Monterey Jack Cheese
1 (4 ounce) can diced green chiles
1 tablespoon minced onion
½ cup milk
1 egg
oil for frying

In a large bowl, combine cornmeal, flour, baking powder, salt, red pepper, Monterey Jack cheese, green chiles, and onions. Stir in milk and egg until just moistened. In a large saucepan, pour oil 3 inches deep. Heat oil to 375 degrees. Drop by tablespoon into oil, fry until golden brown. Drain on paper towel.

Makes 2 dozen

 Mariachi music is the traditional style of music played in Mexico.

Fiery Fast Hushpuppies

1 cup yellow cornmeal
3/4 teaspoon baking powder
1/4 cup milk
1 egg
1 teaspoon chopped green onion
1 teaspoon canned chopped green chiles

In a medium bowl, combine all ingredients. Drop by tablespoons into hot oil. Fry until golden brown. Drain on paper towel.

Makes 1 dozen

The Mexican Hat Dance is also known as a courtship dance.

Manzana Scones

Preheat oven to 425 degrees

2 cups flour
1/4 cup sugar
2 teaspoons baking powder
1/2 teaspoon baking soda
1/2 teaspoon salt
1/4 cup butter, chilled
1/2 cup milk
1 apple, peeled, cored, shredded
2 tablespoons milk
2 tablespoons sugar
1/2 teaspoon cinnamon

In a large bowl, combine flour, 1/4 cup sugar, baking powder, baking soda, and salt. Cut in butter until crumbly. Stir in milk and apple, mix well. On a lightly floured surface, knead dough 10 times. Roll out 2 round 6 inch circles to 1 inch thickness. Cut in pie shapes. Brush tops with 2 tablespoons milk, sprinkle with sugar and cinnamon. Place on a lightly greased baking sheet. Bake for 15 minutes or until golden.

Makes 12 servings

Mexican Sticky Buns

Preheat oven to 375 degrees

1 cup milk
6 tablespoons butter
1 (.25 ounce) package active dry yeast
2 eggs
1/3 cup sugar
1 teaspoon salt
5 cups flour

In a small saucepan, heat milk until first signs of boiling. Remove from heat, add butter, stir until it melts. Transfer milk mixture to a large bowl, cool. Dissolve yeast in milk mixture. Mix in eggs, sugar, salt, and flour 1/2 cup at a time, mixing well after each addition. On a lightly floured surface, knead dough until it is smooth. Lightly oil a large bowl, place dough in bowl and turn to coat with oil. Cover with a damp cloth and set in a warm place to rise. Let rise for 1 hour or until it has doubled in size. Divide dough into 16 equal balls. On a lightly floured surface, roll dough into an oval shape. Place on a lightly greased baking sheet, cover and let rise 45 minutes or until doubled in size.

Topping:
2/3 cup flour
1/2 cup sugar
4 tablespoons butter, softened
2 egg yokes

In a small bowl, combine flour, sugar, butter, and egg yolk. Mix until crumbly. Sprinkle on top of rolls. Bake for 20 minutes or until golden brown.

Makes 16 buns

Many of the folk dances still performed in Mexico originated in pre-Colombian times.

Sopaipillas

2 cups flour
3 teaspoons baking powder
2 tablespoons sugar
1 teaspoon salt
2 tablespoons vegetable shortening
1 cup milk
oil for frying

In a large bowl, combine flour, baking powder, sugar, and salt. Cut in shortening. Stir in milk; mix until a firm ball is formed. On a lightly floured surface, knead dough until smooth. Cover and let rest for 20 minutes. Roll to 1/3 inch thickness. Use a large cookie cutter to make round shapes. In a large skillet, place vegetable oil to a 1/2 inch depth, heat over high heat. Fry sopaipillas to a golden brown. Place on paper towel to drain. Serve with honey or cinnamon and sugar.

Makes 24

Honey is good for one year, whether opened or not.

Treats to Tame

Cakes, Pies, Cookies & Desserts

Salsa Spice Cake

Preheat oven to 350 degrees

2 cups all-purpose flour
1 1/3 cups sugar
4 teaspoons baking powder
1 teaspoon baking soda
3/4 teaspoon cinnamon
1/2 teaspoon ground cloves
1/2 teaspoon allspice
1 cup mild salsa
1/2 cup shortening
2 eggs
1/3 cup water
1 recipe of Easy Cream Cheese Frosting

In a large mixing bowl, combine flour, sugar, baking powder, baking soda, cinnamon, cloves, and allspice. Add salsa and shortening. Beat 3 minutes or until well mixed. Beat in eggs and water. Grease and flour two 8 inch round cake pans. Pour batter into prepared pans, spread evenly. Bake for 30 minutes. Cool and frost with Easy Cream Cheese Frosting.

Easy Cream Cheese Frosting

8 ounces cream cheese,
   room temperature
4 cups powdered sugar
2 tablespoons butter or margarine,
   room temperature
1/2 teaspoon vanilla

In a medium bowl combine all ingredients together. Mix until smooth.

Add a pinch of baking soda to your frosting to keep it moist and prevent cracking.

Chaves Cottage Cheese Cake

Preheat oven to 350 degrees

1 (18¼ ounce) package yellow cake mix
2 pounds cottage cheese
¾ cup sugar
4 eggs
¼ teaspoon vanilla

In a large bowl prepare cake mix according to package directions. Pour batter into a greased and floured 9 x 13 inch baking pan. In a medium bowl, combine cottage cheese, sugar, eggs, and vanilla. Pour cottage cheese mixture evenly over cake batter; do not mix. Bake for 1 hour.

A piñata is a hollow decoration stuffed with candy and is suspended from above. Children are blindfolded and given a stick to swing at the piñata and try to break it.

Blanco Butterscotch Cake

Preheat oven to 350 degrees

2 cups milk
1 (4 ounce) box cook and serve vanilla pudding
1 yellow cake mix
1 (21 ounce) package butterscotch morsels

In a large saucepan, bring milk and pudding to a boil. Remove from heat, stir in cake mix. Pour batter into a greased 9 x 13 inch baking dish. Evenly sprinkle butterscotch morsels on top of batter. Bake for 30 minutes.

Platano Cake

Preheat oven to 350 degree

¹/₂ cup butter, softened
1²/₃ cups sugar
2 eggs
²/₃ cup milk
2¹/₂ cups flour
1¹/₄ teaspoons baking powder
1¹/₄ teaspoons baking soda
¹/₄ teaspoon salt
3 ripe bananas, mashed
1 recipe Cream Cheese Icing *(page 235)*

In a large bowl, cream butter and sugar. Add eggs one at a time, mix well after each addition. Stir in milk. In a small bowl, combine all dry ingredients. Gradually add dry ingredients to butter mixture, mix well. Stir in bananas, mix well. Grease and flour a 9 x 13 inch baking pan. Pour batter into pan. Bake for 30 minutes or until lightly golden brown. Cool and frost.

 Once the piñata is broken, all the children run to get the candy and toys that fall out.

Mexican Fruitcake

Preheat oven to 350 degrees

2 cups flour
2 cups sugar
2 teaspoons baking soda
1 cup chopped chestnuts
20 ounces crushed pineapple with juice
2 eggs

In a large bowl combine flour, sugar, and baking soda. Add remaining ingredients and mix well. Grease a 9 x 13 inch pan, do not flour. Pour batter into pan and bake for 40 minutes. Cool and frost with Easy Cream Cheese Frosting.

Piñatas were originally imported from Italy.

Odessa Cake

Preheat oven to 300 degrees

1 (18¼ ounce) package yellow cake mix
4 eggs
½ cup vegetable oil
1 (4 ounce) can mandarin oranges slices, with juice

Frosting:
1 (15 ounce) can crushed pineapple
1 (4 ounce) box vanilla instant pudding
1 (12 ounce) container whipped topping, thawed

In a large bowl combine cake mix, eggs, and oil. Mix well. Fold oranges and juice into cake batter. Grease and flour 3, 8 inch round cake pans. Pour batter evenly into cake pans. Bake 25 minutes. Top of cake will feel moist. In a medium bowl, combine pineapple, pudding, and whipped topping. Refrigerate frosting for 30 minutes. Frost cake when cooled.

Caramel Cake

Preheat oven to 375 degrees

1 pound light brown sugar
1/2 cup butter or margarine, softened
1 cup flour
1 teaspoon baking powder
1 teaspoon salt
1 1/2 teaspoons vanilla
4 eggs
1 cup chopped pecans
Whipped topping

In a large bowl, cream sugar and butter. In a small bowl, combine flour, baking powder, and salt. Add flour mixture to butter mixture, mix well. Stir in vanilla and eggs. Add pecans and mix well. Pour batter into a lightly greased 9 x 13 inch baking pan. Bake for 30 minutes. Cool and cut into squares. Top with whipped topping.

 You can use a strand of uncooked spaghetti instead of a toothpick to test the doneness of a cake.

Bernalillo Blackberry Jam Cake

Preheat oven to 350 degree

2 cups sugar
1¹/₂ cups butter or margarine
¹/₂ cup buttermilk
4 cups flour
1 teaspoon baking soda
1 teaspoon cinnamon
1 teaspoon nutmeg
1 teaspoon allspice
6 eggs
2 cups blackberry jam

In a large bowl, cream sugar and butter until fluffy. Stir in buttermilk. In a small bowl, combine all dry ingredients. Add flour mixture to butter mixture, mix well. Add eggs 1 at a time, mixing well after each addition. Fold in jam. Grease and flour a 9 x 13 inch baking pan. Bake for 1 hour.

Keep holes and tunnels out of your cake by running a knife through the batter after pouring it into the pan.

Corn Cake

Preheat oven to 350 degrees

1 (17 ounce) can cream corn
$1/2$ cup brown sugar
$3/4$ cup sugar
3 eggs
1 cup corn oil
$1/2$ cup raisins
$1/2$ cup pecans, chopped
$2 1/4$ cups flour
3 teaspoons baking powder
1 teaspoon baking soda
1 teaspoon cinnamon
1 teaspoon salt

In a large bowl, combine corn and sugars. Beat in eggs 1 at a time. Stir in oil. Add raisins and pecans, mix well. In a small bowl combine dry ingredients. Add dry ingredients to corn mixture. Pour batter into a lightly greased 9 x 13 inch baking pan. Bake 40 minutes or until a tooth pick inserted comes out clean. Frost with your choice of icing.

A Roman version of cheesecake first appeared in Cato, Circa 2 B.C.

Pistachio Cheesecake

1 (14 ounce) can sweetened
   condensed milk
1 (4 ounce) box pistachio instant
   pudding
1 (8 ounce) package cream cheese,
   softened
$1/3$ cup lemon juice
1 prepared graham cracker crust

In a large bowl, combine all ingredients, mix well. Pour pistachio mixture into graham cracker crust. Chill for at least 1 hour before serving.

Café Cheesecake

Preheat oven to 375 degrees

**3 (8 ounce) packages cream cheese,
  softened**
4 eggs
1 cup sugar
1 teaspoon vanilla
1/2 cup instant coffee
1 prepared graham cracker crust
whipped topping

In a large bowl, mix cream cheese until fluffy. Add eggs 1 at a time, mixing well after each edition. Stir in sugar, vanilla, and coffee, mix well. Pour cheese mixture into graham cracker crust. Bake for 45 minutes or until almost set in the center. Chill for at least 3 hours. Top with whipped topping before serving.

Mexico City Cheesecakes

Preheat oven to 375 degrees

**2 (8 ounce) packages cream cheese,
  softened**
3/4 cup sugar
2 eggs
1 teaspoon vanilla
vanilla wafers

In a large bowl, combine cream cheese, sugar, eggs, and vanilla, mix well. Line muffin pan with cupcake liners, place a vanilla wafer in the bottom of each cup. Fill each cup 3/4 full with cream cheese mixture. Bake for 15 minutes or until lightly golden brown. Chill before serving.

Traditional piñata saying: Gold and silver do not matter. All I want is to break the piñata.

Playas Peanut Butter Cupcakes

Preheat oven to 350 degrees

1³/4 cups flour
1 cup milk
¹/2 cup peanut butter
¹/4 cup shortening
1 tablespoon baking powder
³/4 teaspoon vanilla
¹/2 teaspoon salt
2 eggs

In a large bowl, combine all ingredients, mix well. Line muffin pan with cupcake liners. Fill each cup ³/4 full. Bake for 20 minutes or until an inserted toothpick comes out clean. Top with chocolate frosting when cool.

Los Lunas Lime Pie

2 (8 ounce) packages cream cheese
1 teaspoon grated lime peel
1 (12 ounce) can sweetened
  condensed milk
1 (8 inch) ready made graham
  cracker crust

In a large bowl, combine cream cheese, lime peel, and milk. Mix with an electric mixer until smooth. Pour into piecrust. Cover and freeze for 6 hours.

Key Lime Pie is a post Civil War recipe.

Dona Ana Apple Pie

Preheat oven to 425 degrees

2 (9 inch) pie crusts, with top crust
1 cup honey
2 tablespoons flour
1 teaspoon cinnamon
1/8 teaspoon salt
6 cups apples, peeled and sliced
1 teaspoon lemon juice
2 teaspoons butter

In a small bowl, combine honey, flour, cinnamon, and salt. Pour half of mixture into the piecrusts. Arrange apples over mixture, pour remainder of honey mixture over apples. Sprinkle lemon juice over each pie and dot with butter. Place top crust over pies and seal edges; cut vents into top crust. Bake for 35 minutes.

Chill pastry dough before rolling it out to keep it from shrinking.

Portales Peach Pie

Preheat oven to 375 degrees

2 (29 ounce) cans sliced peaches, drained
1 cup flour
1 1/2 cups brown sugar, lightly packed
1 1/2 teaspoons ground cinnamon
1 1/2 cups butter or margarine

In a lightly greased deep 9 inch pie pan, place peaches. In a medium bowl combine flour, brown sugar, and cinnamon. Cut butter in until well blended. Sprinkle evenly over peaches. Bake for 25 minutes. Serve warm or cooled.

Soda Pie

3/4 cup sugar
1/2 cup butter
4 tablespoons cocoa
3 eggs
1 prepared graham cracker crust
2 cups whipped topping

In a large bowl, cream sugar, butter, and cocoa for 5 minutes. Add eggs one at a time, beating 5 minutes after each addition. Pour filling into pie crust, chill for at least 1 hour. Top with whipped topping before serving.

Caramel Pecan Pie

1 (4 ounce) box unflavored gelatin
1/4 cup water
1/2 pound vanilla caramel candies
3/4 cup milk
1 cup heavy cream
1/2 cup pecans, chopped
1 teaspoon vanilla
1 prepared graham cracker crust

In a small bowl, combine gelatin and water. In a large saucepan over low heat, melt caramels in milk. Add gelatin to caramels. Remove from heat and cool. Fold in cream, pecans, and vanilla. Pour into crust. Chill for at least 3 hours before serving.

Store nuts in the refrigerator to keep them fresh longer.

Old Mexico Wedding Cookies

Preheat oven to 350 degrees

1 pound unsalted butter
1 cup confectioner's sugar,
   plus extra for dusting
2 tablespoons vanilla extract
1 teaspoon salt
2 cups finely chopped pecans
5 cups sifted cake flour

In a large bowl beat together butter and confectioner's sugar until light and fluffy. Mix in vanilla, salt, and pecans. Using a wooden spoon, stir in flour, do not over mix. Form dough into the size of a small walnut, place on a buttered baking sheet. Bake for 10 or 12 minutes, or until lightly golden brown on bottoms. When cookies are almost cool, roll in powdered sugar

Makes 50 cookies

The traditional shape of the piñata is the six pointed star.

Mexican Chocolate Chip Cookies

Preheat oven to 350 degrees

1 cup butter, softened
1/2 cup confectioner's sugar
2 teaspoons cinnamon
1 teaspoon vanilla
2 cups flour
1 (12 ounce) bag semi-sweet
  chocolate chips
2/3 cup finely chopped walnuts

In a large bowl, cream butter and sugar until creamy and fluffy. Stir in cinnamon and vanilla. Gradually add flour, mixing well. Add 1 1/2 cups chocolate chips and nuts, mix well. Roll dough into 1 inch balls. Place balls on ungreased baking sheet. Bake for 12 minutes or until golden brown. While cookies are cooling, microwave remaining chocolate chips for 40 seconds or until completely melted. Using a spoon, drizzle melted chocolate over each cookie. Refrigerate until chocolate is set.

Makes 2 dozen

 The original chocolate chip cookie recipe was invented in 1930.

Anise Cookies

Preheat oven to 350 degrees

2 3/4 cups flour
2 tablespoons cornstarch
1/2 teaspoon salt
2/3 cup butter or margarine,
   room temperature
1/2 cup shortening
1/2 cup brown sugar, lightly packed
1/2 teaspoon anise seed, crushed
1/3 cup chopped pecans
1/2 package dry active yeast
1/2 cup warm water

In a large bowl, combine flour, cornstarch, and salt. In a small bowl cream butter and shortening, add sugar. Add to flour and mix. Add anise seeds and pecans, mix. Dissolve yeast evenly in warm water. Blend yeast into flour mixture until soft dough forms. Form dough into a roll and cut in half. Cut 10 to 12 cookies from each roll. Round and flatten out a bit on an ungreased cookie sheet. Bake for 25 minutes.

Makes 24 cookies

To soften brown sugar, add a slice of soft white bread to the container and close tightly. After a few hours it will be soft again.

Costilla Cake Cookies

Preheat oven to 350 degrees

1 (18 1/4 ounce) cake mix, flavor of choice
2 eggs
1/2 cup oil

In a large bowl, combine all ingredients; mix well. Drop dough by tablespoon, 2 inches apart, on a lightly greased baking sheet. Bake for 8 to 10 minutes or until golden brown. Cool before serving.

Makes 2 dozen cookies

Black Pepper Cookies

Preheat oven to 350 degrees

2¹/₂ cups flour
¹/₂ teaspoon black pepper
2 teaspoons baking powder
2¹/₂ teaspoons ginger
1 teaspoon cinnamon
¹/₂ teaspoon allspice
1 cup sugar
¹/₂ cup butter
1 egg
1 tablespoon vanilla

In a small bowl mix flour, black pepper, baking powder, ginger, cinnamon, and allspice. In a large bowl beat sugar and butter until light and fluffy. Beat in eggs and vanilla. Gradually beat in flour mixture. Chill dough for 1 hour. Make a 2¹/₂ inch roll and cut in slices. Bake for 10 minutes.

Makes 18 cookies

 Cookie dough can be frozen for up to 3 months or refrigerated for 3 or 4 days.

Mexican Sun Cookies

Preheat oven to 350 degrees

1 cup butter or margarine, softened
1/2 cup brown sugar, packed light
11/2 cups sugar
1 egg
1 tablespoon grated orange peel
21/4 cups flour
3/4 teaspoon baking soda
1/2 teaspoon salt
11/2 cup vanilla chips

In a large bowl cream butter and sugars. Add egg and orange peel, mix well. In a small bowl mix flour, baking soda, and salt. Gradually add flour mixture to butter mixture, mix well. Blend in vanilla chips. Drop by teaspoon 2 inches apart on to an ungreased baking sheet. Bake for 10 minutes or until golden brown.

Makes 3 dozen

Sugar does not spoil, but may change in flavor.

Spanish Peanut Cookies

2 (6 ounce) packages semi-sweet
  chocolate
1 cup Spanish peanuts
2 cups chow mein noodles

In a large saucepan over low heat, melt chocolate. Gradually stir in peanuts and chow mein noodles. Drop by teaspoon onto wax paper. Refrigerate 15 minutes.

Makes 2 dozen

La Plata Pecan Cookies

Preheat over to 325 degrees

**1 cup real butter (no substitutes),
  softened**
1/2 cup sugar
1 teaspoon vanilla
2 cups flour
1 cup finely chopped pecans
confectioner's sugar, for dusting

In a medium bowl, cream butter, sugar,
and vanilla. Gradually add flour and pecans,
mix well. Drop rounded teaspoon size dough
on an ungreased cookie sheet 1 inch apart.
Bake for 20 to 24 minutes or until lightly
golden brown. Let cool on cookie sheet
slightly before moving. Dust with
confectioner's sugar.

Makes 6 dozen

Cozumel Coconut Cookies

Preheat oven to 350 degrees

1 1/3 cups sweetened condensed milk
1 teaspoon vanilla
1/4 teaspoon salt
3 cups shredded coconut

In a medium bowl combine milk, vanilla,
and salt. Stir in coconut. Drop by teaspoon
onto a lightly greased baking sheet. Bake
for 10 minutes

Makes 2 1/2 dozen

Do not substitute light or reduced fat margarine for regular margarine or butter. Light and reduced fat margarine contains extra moistener.

Ozona Oatmeal Cookies

Preheat oven to 350 degrees

1 cup flour
1 cup rolled oats
1/2 cup sugar
1 teaspoon cinnamon
1/2 teaspoon salt
1/2 teaspoon baking soda
1/2 teaspoon baking powder
3/4 cup raisins
1/3 cup corn syrup
2 egg whites
1 teaspoon vanilla extract

In a large bowl, combine flour, oats, sugar, cinnamon, salt, baking soda, and baking powder. Add remaining ingredients, stir well. Drop by rounded teaspoons onto cookie sheet. Bake for 8 to 10 minutes.

Makes 30 cookies

Vanilla: A study showed if you use imitation or real vanilla, the baking results will be the same.

Peco Peanut Butter Cookies

Preheat oven to 375 degrees

1²/₃ cups flour
1¹/₂ tablespoons cornstarch
1³/₄ teaspoons baking powder
¹/₂ teaspoon baking soda
³/₄ cup brown sugar, firmly packed
¹/₄ cup sugar
¹/₄ cup creamy peanut butter
¹/₄ cup vegetable oil
1¹/₂ tablespoons light colored corn syrup
2¹/₂ teaspoons vanilla extract
1 egg
3 tablespoons sugar

In a medium size bowl, combine flour, cornstarch, baking powder, and baking soda, set aside. In a large bowl, mix brown sugar, ¹/₄ cup sugar, peanut butter, and oil, blend on medium speed of mixer until well blended. Add corn syrup, vanilla, and egg, beat well. Stir in flour mixture, mix well. Coat hands with cooking spray and shape 48, 1 inch balls. Roll in the 3 tablespoons sugar and place on a cookie sheet 2 inches apart. Using a fork, make criss cross marks on top of cookies to flatten slightly. Bake for 8 minutes.

Makes 48 cookies

Self Rising Flour is 1 cup All Purpose Flour with 1¹/₂ teaspoons baking powder and ¹/₂ teaspoon of salt added.

Patata Cookies

Preheat oven to 325 degrees

1 cup sugar
1 cup brown sugar
1 cup butter
2 eggs
1 cup flour
1 teaspoon baking soda
1 teaspoon salt
1 cup crushed potato chips

In a large bowl, cream sugars and butter until fluffy. Add eggs, mix well. Stir in flour gradually. Add soda and salt, mix well. Add potato chips, mix well. Refrigerate dough for 1 hour. Roll into 1 inch balls and place on an ungreased baking sheet. Press the top of the cookie with a small glass. Bake for 10 minutes or until slightly brown around the edges.

Makes 2 dozen

If you use unsalted butter when making cookies, they will have a lighter texture.

Polvorone Cookies

Preheat oven to 350 degrees

**3 tablespoons blanched slivered
  almonds**
1³/4 cups flour
6 tablespoons sugar
1/4 teaspoon cinnamon
6 tablespoons butter or margarine
1 tablespoon powdered sugar

In a large skillet over high heat, toast
almonds until golden brown. Finely crush
almonds, set aside. In the same skillet over
medium heat, brown flour until golden, set
aside to cool. In a large bowl, combine
almonds, flour, sugar, and cinnamon. Add
butter and mix until a firm dough forms. Roll
dough out to a 1/4 inch, cut into 2 inch circles.
Place cookies on a greased baking sheet.
Bake for 15 minutes. Dust cookies with
powdered sugar and cool.

Makes 1 dozen

All Purpose Flour is made from hard and soft wheat.

Siete Layer Bars

Preheat oven to 325 degrees

1/4 pound butter
1 cup graham cracker crumbs
1 cup chocolate chips
1 cup coconut
1 cup walnuts, chopped
1 cup butterscotch chips
1 cup sweetened condensed milk

Melt butter in a 9 x 13 inch pan; spread
evenly in bottom of pan. Layer ingredients
in order over butter. Pour milk gently over
top. Bake for 25 minutes. Cut into squares.

Makes 24 bars

Coffee Bars

Preheat oven to 325 degrees

2 teaspoons instant coffee granules
1 teaspoon vanilla
3/4 cup brown sugar, packed
1 cup butter, room temperature
2 1/2 cups flour
1/4 teaspoon cinnamon
1/8 teaspoon salt

Filling:
1/4 cup sweetened condensed milk
3 ounces white chocolate, chopped
1/2 teaspoon vanilla topping
2 ounces milk chocolate, melted

Fresh milled flour is light yellow in color. It is bleached to lighten the color.

In a small bowl, dissolve coffee in the vanilla. In a large bowl, beat sugar and butter until fluffy. Beat in coffee mixture. In a medium bowl, combine flour, cinnamon, and salt. Blend into batter, mix well. Divide in half and flatten into 6 circles. Place wax paper between layers and on top and bottom. Chill 1 hour. In a small saucepan, heat over low, condensed milk, white chocolate, and vanilla until chocolate is melted. Cool 5 minutes

Remove dough from refrigerator and roll into a 6 x 14 inch rectangle. Over half of each rectangle pour milk and chocolate mixture, do not pour mixture to the edge, leave a 1/2 inch border around each rectangle. Fold the section of dough without the filling over section with filling, press edges to seal. Place dough on a cookie sheet and refrigerate for an additional 30 minutes. Bake for 35 minutes or until golden brown on bottom. Let cool then cut into 2 inch bars. Drizzle melted milk chocolate over top of bars.

Makes 25 bars

Arroz Pudding

Preheat oven to 300 degrees

4 cups milk
1/2 cup rice
1 cup heavy whipping cream
2/3 cup sugar
1 teaspoon vanilla
1/2 teaspoon salt

In a medium saucepan, scald milk. Place rice in a 2 quart baking dish. Cover rice with milk, bake for 2 hours, stir occasionally. Remove from oven, add cream, sugar, vanilla, and salt, mix well. Serve warm or cold.

Makes 6 servings

Choco Arroz Pudding

3 cups cooked rice
1 1/2 cups sour cream
1/2 cup sugar
2 tablespoons cocoa powder
1 tablespoon flour
1 1/2 teaspoons vanilla

In a large saucepan over medium heat, combine all ingredients. Cook for 5 minutes. Serve hot or cold.

Makes 6 servings

Butter stays fresh in the refrigerator for up to 2 weeks. Margarine will stay fresh for up to 6 months in the refrigerator.

Rio Arriba Rice Pudding

2 cups water
1/2 teaspoon salt
1/2 cup rice
1 (4 ounce) box vanilla pudding
  (not instant)

In a medium saucepan bring water and salt to a boil. Add rice and cook until rice is soft. Prepare pudding according to package instructions. Stir prepared pudding into rice, mix well. Serve warm or cold.

Makes 6 servings

Meloso Rice Pudding

Preheat oven to 300 degrees

4 cups milk
1/2 cup long grain rice
1/2 cup raisins
1/4 cup honey
1/2 teaspoon salt
1/2 teaspoon vanilla
1/2 teaspoon cinnamon

In a 1 1/2 quart saucepan, combine all ingredients except cinnamon. Bake uncovered for 2 hours, stirring every 20 minutes. Top with cinnamon. Serve warm or cold.

Makes 6 servings

Insert a toothpick in the center of a cake, if it comes out clean the cake is done.

Luna Lemon Pudding

Preheat oven to 350 degrees

1¹/2 cups sugar
¹/2 cup flour
¹/2 teaspoon baking powder
¹/4 teaspoon salt
3 eggs, separated
1¹/2 cups milk
¹/4 cup lemon juice
2 teaspoons grated lemon rind
2 tablespoons butter, melted

In a large bowl, combine 1 cup sugar, flour, baking powder, and salt, set aside. In a small bowl, beat egg whites until stiff. Gradually add remaining ¹/2 cup sugar, mix well, set aside. In a medium bowl, beat egg yolks. Add milk, lemon juice, lemon rind, and butter to yolks, mix well. Stir egg yolk mixture into flour mixture, mix well. Fold in egg white mixture. Pour into a 2 quart baking dish. Bake for 45 minutes. Chill before serving.

Makes 6 servings

 Lemon meringue pie was created in Philadelphia in the early 1800's.

Buena Vista Blueberry Bread Pudding

Preheat oven to 350 degrees

1/4 cup butter
1/2 teaspoon cinnamon
6 cups dried bread cubes
1 1/2 cups apricot flavored syrup
2 teaspoons lemon peel
2 tablespoons lemon juice
1/4 cup water
3/4 cup chopped pecans
1/2 pound Monterey Jack cheese,
** cut into 1/2 inch cubes**
1 1/2 cups blueberries,
** rinsed and drained**

Place butter and cinnamon in a 9 x 13 inch baking dish. Bake until butter is melted, stir to mix. Place bread cubes in baking dish. In a small bowl, combine apricot syrup, lemon peel, lemon juice, and water. Pour mixture over bread and mix well. Add pecans and cheese, mix well. Gently fold in blueberries, distribute ingredients evenly. Cover completely with foil. Bake for 20 minutes. Uncover and bake for an additional 15 minutes.

Makes 12 servings

To keep a bowl from slipping and sliding place a damp towel under the bowl.

Belen Bread Pudding

Preheat oven to350 degrees

2 cups cream
6 slices day old bread
1 cup sugar
1 teaspoon vanilla
1 teaspoon cinnamon
1 tablespoon butter, melted
3 eggs, slightly beaten
1 tablespoon flour
1/4 teaspoon nutmeg

In a large bowl, pour cream over day old bread, let soak for 10 minutes. Add remaining ingredients, mix well. Pour into a greased 2 quart baking dish. Bake for 30 minutes or until golden brown. Serve with sauce

Sauce:
1 cup water
1 tablespoon flour
1/2 cup sugar
2 tablespoons butter
1 teaspoon vanilla

In a small saucepan over medium heat, combine all ingredients. Simmer 10 minutes.

Makes 8 servings

 To refrigerate egg yolks, cover with cold water and refrigerate.

Flan

Preheat oven to 350 degrees

3/4 cup sugar
**1 (14 ounce) can sweetened
  condensed milk**
1 cup whipping cream
1/2 cup milk
4 eggs
1 cinnamon stick

Condensed milk was first manufactured in 1858.

Heat sugar in a small skillet over medium high heat. Reduce heat to medium when sugar begins to melt, stirring often. When sugar has browned, spoon over bottom and sides of a shallow 1½ quart baking dish. Set aside to cool. In a blender, combine condensed milk, whipping cream, milk and eggs, until well blended. Pour milk mixture into baking dish lined with caramelized sugar. Drop cinnamon stick into middle. Place baking dish containing the flan, into a larger deeper baking pan. Pour enough hot water into baking dish to cover half way up side of the dish containing the flan. Bake for 1 hour and 50 minutes or until
a knife inserted off center comes out clean. Remove baking dish from water, cool then refrigerate for 3 hours. Serve the flan upside-down on a platter.

Makes 6 servings

Caramel Flan

Preheat oven to 350 degrees

5 eggs
1/2 cup sugar
1 teaspoon vanilla
1/8 teaspoon salt
2 1/2 cups milk
6 teaspoons caramel ice cream topping

In a medium bowl, lightly beat eggs. Add sugar, vanilla, and salt. Stir in milk, mix well. Place one teaspoon caramel topping into 6 ungreased 6 ounce custard cups. Place custard cups in a 13 x 9 x 2 inch baking pan. Pour egg mixture into cups. Add hot water to the baking pan until it is one inch deep. Bake uncovered for 30 to 35 minutes or until center of each is almost set. Remove from water and cool. Refrigerate for at least 3 hours. Turn upside down and unmold onto individual serving dishes.

Makes 6 servings

Chill pastry dough before rolling it out to keep it from shrinking.

Apple Quesadillas

Preheat oven to 400 degrees

2 (6 inch) tortillas
1/4 cup chunky applesauce
1 tablespoon sugar, divided
1/2 teaspoon cinnamon, divided
1/4 cup shredded cheddar cheese

Place 1 tortilla on an ungreased baking sheet. Spread 1/4 cup apple sauce on tortilla. Sprinkle half of sugar and cinnamon over applesauce. Top with cheese. Place remaining tortilla on top and sprinkle remaining sugar and cinnamon on top. Bake for 8 minutes or until golden brown. Cut into pie shaped pieces and serve.

Makes 4 servings

Cheesy Apple Quesadillas

Preheat oven to 350 degrees

1 (21 ounce) can apple pie filling
1/3 cup raisins
1/2 teaspoon ground cinnamon
8 (6 inch) flour tortillas
1 1/2 cups shredded cheddar cheese

In a medium size bowl, combine apple pie filling, raisins, and cinnamon. Coat a large skillet with cooking spray. Heat over medium high heat. Place one tortilla in skillet. Top with 2 tablespoons of cheese followed by 1/4 cup apple pie mixture. Cook 2 minutes or until cheese is melted and the tortilla is a golden brown. Fold tortilla in half and remove from skillet placing it on a baking sheet. Repeat process until all tortillas are used. Sprinkle remaining cheese over top of folded tortillas and bake for 3 minutes. Cut each tortilla into 3 wedges each.

Makes 24

Use fresh fruit and vegetbles within five weeks. Store them in their original cartons and do not wash until the time of use

Apple Enchilada

Preheat oven to 350 degrees

6 (8 inch) flour tortillas
1 (21 ounce) can apple pie filling
1/2 cup brown sugar
1/2 cup sugar
1/2 cup water
1/3 cup butter or margarine
1 teaspoon cinnamon

On each tortilla, spoon pie filling spreading evenly. Roll up tortillas and place seam side down in a lightly greased 8 x 8 inch baking dish. In a medium saucepan bring sugars, water, butter, and cinnamon to a boil. Reduce heat and simmer until sugar is dissolved. Pour mixture over tortillas. Bake for 20 minutes.

Makes 6 servings

 Store ripe bananas in the refrigerator. The skin will turn brown but the banana will stay fresh.

Banana Chimichangas

3 bananas, sliced
1/2 cup brown sugar
1/4 cup butter or margarine
1 teaspoon vanilla
2 (10 inch) flour tortillas
vegetable oil for frying

In a large skillet over medium heat, sauté bananas and brown sugar in butter until sugar is dissolved. Reduce heat; stir in vanilla and cook for 1 minute. Divide banana mixture between the tortillas. Fold ends over and roll closed. In a large skillet heat 1 inch of vegetable oil. Fry tortillas until golden brown. Drain on a paper towel. Serve warm

Makes 2 servings

Churros

1/2 cup butter or margarine
1/4 teaspoon salt
1 cup water
1 cup flour
3 eggs
1/4 cup sugar
1/4 teaspoon cinnamon
Vegetable oil

In a large saucepan, over high heat add butter, salt, and water to a rolling boil. Reduce heat to low and add flour. Mix until mixture forms a ball, about one minute. Remove from heat and add eggs all at once, beat until smooth. In a medium bowl, mix sugar and cinnamon. Spoon mixture into decorators' tube with a large star tip. In a large skillet, heat vegetable oil to 360 degrees. Squeeze a 4 inch strip of dough into hot oil. Fry 3 to four strips at a time until golden brown on all sides. Drain on a paper towel. Roll in sugar and cinnamon mixture.

Makes 24

Dip the measuring cup in water before measuring butter or shortening. It will not stick to the cup and will come out in one piece.

Fried Ice Cream

1 cup vegetable oil
2 cups crushed frosted flakes
4 scoops vanilla ice cream
2 cups confectioner's sugar
2 teaspoons cinnamon

Heat oil in a medium saucepan over high heat. Place crushed frosted flakes in a large bowl. Roll ice cream scoop in flakes until well coated. Place coated ice cream in hot oil for 30 to 40 seconds. Take ice cream out of oil and dust with confectioner's sugar and cinnamon. Repeat process three more times. Serve immediately.

Makes 4 servings

Carmel Bananas

4 tablespoons brown sugar
2 tablespoons butter
4 ripe bananas, peeled

In a small saucepan over low heat, combine brown sugar and butter. Cook until sugar is melted. Place bananas in a microwaveable baking dish, pour brown sugar mixture over top. Microwave for 1 minute. Serve with vanilla ice cream.

Makes 4 servings

Queso Treat

Preheat oven to 350 degrees

1 pound mozzarella cheese
2 cups dark brown sugar
1 cup water
1 teaspoon cinnamon

Cut cheese into ¼ inch slices. Arrange in a lightly greased 8 x 8 inch pan. In a small saucepan, bring sugar, water, and cinnamon to a boil. Boil for 5 minutes. Pour sugar mixture over cheese. Bake for 10 minutes.

Makes12 servings

 Do not store bananas with apples. The apples will make the bananas ripen quicker.

Cereza Dessert

Preheat oven to 350 degrees

**1¹/₂ cups sugar
1 cup butter or margarine
4 eggs
1 teaspoon vanilla
2 cups flour
2 teaspoons baking powder
1 (21 ounce) can cherry pie filling
1 (9 ounce) container whipped topping**

In a large bowl, cream sugar and butter. Mix in eggs and vanilla until fluffy. Add flour and baking powder, mix well. Pour batter into a lightly greased 9 x 13 inch baking pan. Spoon pie filling evenly over batter. Bake for 45 minutes or until golden brown. Top with whipped topping.

Makes 16 servings

Substitute cherry pie filling for frosting on your next chocolate cake.

Mantecados

Preheat oven to 375 degrees

**1 cup sugar
1 cup butter
6 eggs
2 cups flour
2 tablespoons confectioner's sugar**

In a large bowl, cream 1 cup sugar and butter until fluffy. Add eggs one at a time, mix well. Slowly stir in flour, mix well. Place paper muffin liners into a muffin pan. Pour batter into liners. Sprinkle confectioner's sugar over the top of each. Bake for 15 minutes or until an inserted knife comes out clean.

Makes 8 servings

Manazana Crisp

Preheat oven to 350 degrees

5 cups thinly sliced apples
1 cup brown sugar
3/4 cup quick cooking oats
1 teaspoon cinnamon
1/2 cup butter or margarine
3/4 cup flour

In a 9 x 13 inch baking dish, arrange apples.
In a medium bowl, combine remaining
ingredients, mix well. Press mixture over
apples evenly. Bake for 45 to 50 minutes.

Makes 12 servings

Serving
tip: serve
manazana
crisp warm with
a scoop of
vanilla ice
cream.

Red Hot Dessert

1 cup hot water
1/4 cup cinnamon red hot candies
2 (4 ounce) boxes cherry Jell-O
1 (25 ounce) can applesauce
Whipped topping

Boil water and dissolve red hot candies
in it. Add 1 package of Jell-O and applesauce;
stir until Jell-O dissolves. Pour into 8 X 8 inch
pan. Let stand. Prepare the second package
of plain cherry Jell-O according to package
instructions, pour over bottom layer. Cool
and refrigerate. Top with the whipped
topping.

Makes 10 servings

Raging Red Hot Glass Candy

2 3/4 cups sugar
3/4 cup white Karo syrup
3/4 cup water
1 teaspoon cinnamon oil

In a large saucepan over medium heat, combine sugar, syrup, and water. Bring to a hard boil. Boil 7 minutes. Remove from heat and add cinnamon oil. Pour onto a buttered baking sheet with a lip. Let cool, break into pieces.

Storage tip: layer raging red hot glass candy between layers of wax paper to keep the pieces from sticking together.

Cinnaberry Dessert

1 (3 ounce) package raspberry gelatin
1 cup boiling water
3 tablespoons red hot cinnamon candies
1 cup applesauce

In a medium bowl, dissolve gelatin, water, and candies. Add applesauce. Pour into mold. Refrigerate until set.

Makes 10 servings

index

278

notes:

notes:

notes:

Other Cookbooks Available From Creative Ideas Publishing

To order, fill out enclosed order form.

JUST AROUND THE CURVE by Sharon and Gene McFall. Designed for RVers and Campers, but is great for the home. Over 350 great quick and easy recipes. Recipes from all 50 states. Also contains some low-fat, low-cal and diabetic recipes. Intriguing American points of interest and travel tips and tidbits. A must for the traveler or at home. $16.95.

BUSY WOMAN'S COOKBOOK A national bestseller by Sharon and Gene McFall. Over 350,000 copies sold. It has over 500 mouth-watering 3 and 4 ingredient recipes and more than 200 short stories and facts about famous and influential women.$16.95

COOKIN' WITH WILL ROGERS By Sharon and Gene McFall. Has over 560 delicious country cookin' recipes with over 100 Will Rogers quotes, 60 pictures and 50 stories of one of America's most beloved humorists. "Only a fool argues with a skunk, a mule or a cook." Will Rogers. $19.95.

GET ME OUT OF THE KITCHEN By Sharon and Gene McFall. 500 easy to prepare recipes. Special low-fat and low-cal recipes as well as helpful cooking hints. A wonderful cookbook. $18.95.

IF I GOTTA COOK MAKE IT QUICK By Shelley Plettl. Over 400 delicious crockpot and just a few ingredients recipes. Includes: Helpful Hints and Fun Facts; How to Adapt Your Favorite Recipe to the Crockpot; How to Substitute One Ingredient for Another; Uses of Herbs and Spices; Basic Rules for Table Manners. $18.95.

Coming Soon

JUST NO TIME TO COOK! By Linda Burgett. Over 500 shortcut recipes. Delicious and quick and easy to make with ingredients that are found in any kitchen. It also has special recipes and great ideas for the holidays. This cookbook will simplify your life in the kitchen and during the holidays. $18.95

Please send _____ copies of *Mild to Wild Mexican Cookbook*

@ 18.95 (U.S.) each $ _____

Postage and handling @ $3.50 each $ _____

Texas residents add sales tax @ $1.69 each $ _____

TOTAL $ _____

Check or Credit Card (Canada - credit card only)

Charge to my ☐ Master Card or Visa Card

Account # _____

Expiration Date _____

Signature _____

```
MAIL TO:
B&B Books
P.O. Box 1697
Aztec, NM  87410
800-673-0768
```

Name _____

Address _____

City _____ State _____ Zip _____

Phone (day) _____ (night) _____

ORDER BY EMAIL: cookbooksbylinda@yahoo.com

✂ -

Please send _____ copies of _____

@ _____ (U.S.) each $ _____

Postage and handling @ $3.50 each $ _____

Texas residents add sales tax @ $1.69 each $ _____

TOTAL $ _____

Check or Credit Card (Canada - credit card only)

Charge to my ☐ Master Card or Visa Card

Account # _____

Expiration Date _____

Signature _____

```
MAIL TO:
B&B Books
P.O. Box 1697
Aztec, NM  87410
800-673-0768
```

Name _____

Address _____

City _____ State _____ Zip _____

Phone (day) _____ (night) _____

ORDER BY EMAIL: cookbooksbylinda@yahoo.com

Share Your Favorite Recipes!

Do you have a favorite quick and easy recipe? Do family and friends ask you for it? Would you like to see it in a national cookbook?

If so, please send your favorite quick and easy recipe to us. If we use it in a future cookbook, you will be given credit in the book for the recipe, and will receive a free copy of the book.

Name

Address

Phone

MAIL TO:
B&B Books
P.O. Box 1697
Aztec, NM 87410

Share Your Favorite Recipes!

Do you have a favorite quick and easy recipe? Do family and friends ask you for it? Would you like to see it in a national cookbook?

If so, please send your favorite quick and easy recipe to us. If we use it in a future cookbook, you will be given credit in the book for the recipe, and will receive a free copy of the book.

Name

Address

Phone

MAIL TO:
B&B Books
P.O. Box 1697
Aztec, NM 87410